The Test of Scarlet

The Test of Scarlet

Experiences of an Artillery Officer
During the First World War

Coningsby Dawson

LEONAUR

The Test of Scarlet
Experiences of an Artillery Officer
During the First World War
by Coningsby Dawson

First published under the titles
The Test of Scarlet

Leonaur is an imprint
of Oakpast Ltd

ISBN: 978-0-85706-741-8 (hardcover)
ISBN: 978-0-85706-742-5 (softcover)

http://www.leonaur.com

Contents

CHAPTER 1

The Quiet Before the Storm

The raid is over. The frenzied appeal of the Hun flares has died down. Flares are the deaf and dumb language of the front. Sometimes they say, "We are advancing"; sometimes, "We are beaten back." Most often they say, "We are in danger; call upon the artillery for help." Tonight they seemed to be crying out for mercy—speaking not to friends, but to us. We were silent as God, and now they too are silent.

In the welter of darkness one can still make out the exact location of the enemy's front-line by the glow of his burning dugouts. Our chaps set them on fire, standing in the doorways like avenging angels, and hurling down incendiary bombs as he tried to rush up the stairs. A horrid way to die, imprisoned underground in a raging furnace! Yet at this distance the destruction looks comfortable as the reflection of many campfires about which companions sit and warm their hands. The only companions in those trenches now are Corruption and his old friend Death.

I can see it all—the twisted terror of the bodies, the mangled redness of what once were men. I see these things too clearly—before they happen, while they are happening and when I am not there. It is only when I am there that I do not see them, and they fail to impress me. It was so tonight as I crouched in my observation post, my telephonist beside me, waiting for the show to commence. As the second-hand ticked round to zero hour, I had an overpowering desire to delay the oncoming destruction.

I peopled the enemy line with imaginary characters and built up stories about them. I pictured the homes they had left, the affections, the sweethearts, the little children. God knows why I should pity them. And then our chaps—they are known personalities; I can paint with exact precision the contrast between what they are and what they were. I see them always with laughter in their eyes, however desperate the job in hand.

Their faces lean and eager as bayonets, they assemble in some main trench, as likely as not facetiously named after some favourite actress. On our present front we have the Doris Keane, the Teddie Gerrard and the Gaby. A sharply whispered word of command! They move forward, shuffling along the duckboard, come to the jumping-off point and commence to follow the lanes in the wire which lead out from safety across No Man's Land. They crouch like panthers, flinging themselves flat every time a rocket ascends. Within shouting distance of the enemy, they drop into shell-holes and lie silent. All this I see in my mind as I gaze impotently through the blackness. My turn comes later when the raid is in full swing; it consists in directing the artillery fire and reporting to the rear what is happening.

I consult the illuminated dial of my wristwatch—five seconds to go. Some battery, which has grown nervous, starts pooping off its rounds. A machine-gunner, imitating the bad example, commences a swift *rat-a-tat-tat*: Destiny demanding entrance on the door of some sleeping house. In the wall of darkness, as though a candle had been lighted and a blind pulled aside, a solitary flare ascends—then another, then another. North and south, like panic spreading, the illumination runs. With the clash of an iron door flung wide, all our batteries open up. I look behind me; flash follows flash.

The horizon is lit up from end to end. The gunners are baking their loaves of death. The air is filled with a hissing as of serpents. Shells travel so thick and fast overhead that they seem to jostle and struggle for a passage. The first of them arrive. So far no eye has followed their flight. Suddenly they halt, reined in by their masters at the guns, and plunge snarling and golden on the heads of the enemy. Where a second ago there was blackness, a wall of fire and lead has grown up. Poor devils! Those who escape the shells will be destroyed by bomb and bayonet. Pity there is none; this is the hour of revenge. We shall take three prisoners, perhaps, in order that we may gather information, but the rest.

Our chaps have to think of their own safety. There is only one company in the raid, consisting of not over a hundred men. They might easily be surrounded. Their success depends on the element of surprise and the quickness of their get-away when they have done their work. If they took too many prisoners they would be hampered in their return. If they left any of the enemy alive behind them, they would be fired on as they retired. So the order is "No quarter and kill swiftly."

Now that the attack has started, I cease to be concerned for the Hun: all my thought is for our chaps. I know so many of them. Silborrad, the scout officer of the 11th Battalion is there; a frail appearing lad, with the look of a consumptive and the heart of a lion. It was he who with one sergeant held up sixty Huns at Avion, driving them back with bombs from traverse to traverse. Battling Brown is in charge of the company; he's the champion raiding officer of our corps and, with the exception of the V. C, has won every decoration that a man can earn. Curious stories are told about him. It is said that in the return from one raid he had brought three prisoners within sight of our lines when suddenly, without rhyme or reason, he lined them up and shot them dead.

The moment he had done so he fell to weeping. This particular raid had been put on to gain identifications of the enemy division that was facing us. By killing his prisoners he had failed in the purpose for which the raid had been planned. You cannot wring answers from the dead. Having seen his men safely back into our trenches, he set out alone across No Man's Land. What he did there or how he did it, he has never told to anyone; but by dawn he came padding back through our wire, driving three new prisoners in front of him. For every Hun he shoots he makes a notch in the handle of his revolver. He has used up the handles of three revolvers already.

He's tall and slim as a girl, with nice eyes and a wistful sort of mouth. When he came to the war he was barely eighteen; today he's scarcely twenty-one. War hasn't aged him; he thrives on it and looks, if anything, more boyish. It's only in a fight that his face loses its brooding expression of thwarted tenderness. Of a sudden it becomes hard and stern—almost Satanic. There never was such a man for clutching at glory.

And then there's big Dick Dirk. When he first joined our brigade, he got the reputation for being yellow because he talked so freely about being afraid. He has no right to be in the raid. It isn't his job; he's supposed to be deep underground in the battalion headquarters' dugout, carrying on his duties as liaison-officer. None of the artillery know, except myself, that he intended to go over the top with the infantry tonight. When our colonel learns of his escapade, he'll give him hell.

Dick is six-foot-three, slow in speech, simple as a child and so honest that it hurts. He stoops a little at the shoulders, falls forward at the knees and is as gray as a badger. His expression is worn and kindly, and his lower lip pendulous. You would set him down as stupid, if it were not for the twinkle in his eyes. I don't think Dick ever kissed a girl; he would not consider it honourable and, in any case, holds too humble an opinion of himself. Since he's been at the front he's managed to get engaged to one of his sister's schoolgirl friends.

She's a Brazilian. He knows nothing about her, has never seen her, but like all of us, dreads the loneliness of "going west" without the knowledge that there is one girl who cares. She started the friendship by adding postscripts to his sister's letters. Then she asked that he would send her a photo of himself. For some time he dodged her request, and afterwards spent weeks of wracking nervousness lest his looks should fall below her standards.

Now that he's engaged, he treats the entire war as though it were being fought for her. He still talks of being afraid. He refuses to lie about his sensations. The more he sees of shell-fire the stronger grows his physical dread. Because of this, he continually sets traps for his cowardice. Tonight he set another trap. I suppose he got to thinking how he'd hate to be an infantryman in a raid, so he decided to go over the top with them. At the present moment he might be in England, but cut his leave short, returned from Blighty and was sent up forward as liaison-officer. It was only yesterday that he surprised me by raising the gas-blanket and pushing in his head.

"You!" I exclaimed. "I was picturing you in Piccadilly. What's brought you back from Blighty six days ahead of time?"

He flushed, but his eyes mocked his confusion. "It was devilishly lonely in London," he said slowly; "there were too many girls." And then, with an embarrassed smile, "I wanted to go straight because of her."

So because he wanted to go straight for her, he's out in No Man's Land tonight, retesting his worth and taking his life in his hands. There's a woman at the back of each one of us who inspires most of our daring. With some of us she's the woman whom we hope to meet, with others the woman whom we've met. Whether she lives in the future or the present, we carry on in an effort to be worthy of her. And when it's ended, will she be worthy? Will she guess that we did it all for her? We shall never tell her; if she loves us, she will guess.

A sunken road, rotten with rain and mud, runs twenty yards to my left. I shall know when the raiders return, for I shall hear the weary tread of the wounded and the prisoners as they pass this point. A little higher up the road I can already hear the muffled panting of an ambulance, waiting to carry back the dead. Should I miss them, the quickened beat of the engine will warn me. The enemy knows that this is the route by which they must return; he's lobbing over gas-shells and searching with whizz-bangs. A messy way of spending life! Did God know that it was for this that He was creating us when He launched us on our adventure through the world?

11

CHAPTER 2

No Man's Land

It's morning. We're always safe when the light has come. The most dangerous hour in the twenty-four is the one when day is dawning. Throughout that hour the infantry always "stand to" with rifles, bombs and Lewis guns, on the alert for an attack. S. O. S. rockets are kept handy, so that help can be summoned. At every observation-post an especially keen lookout is kept; at the batteries the sentries stand with eyes fixed on the eastern horizon to catch the first signal of distress.

The anxious hour is over and morning has come. For another day men breathe more freely; till night returns, death has been averted. The narrow slit, just above the level of the ground, through which I spy on the enemy, reveals a green and dewy country. The little flowers of the field are still asleep, their faces covered by their tiny petal-hands. I want to shout to them to wake up and be companionable. After watching many dawns I have discovered that poppies are the early risers among the flowers and that dandelions are the sleepy heads.

The ridge falls away from where I am. Beneath the slope, directly in front, there is a village destroyed by shell-fire. To the right there is another village equally desolate. Still further in front there are two more villages which have been trampled into dust by attacks and counter-attacks. Every tree is dead. Every wood has been uprooted. Every calvary, with its suffering Christ, has been knocked down. When the morning clears I shall be able to see for miles across all the intricate trench system of the

Huns, defence line behind defence line, to the barricade of cities on the eastward edge of the plain. In those cities life seems to follow its normal round.

The clock in the town hall of Douai is so accurate that we can set our watches by it. Plumes of smoke puff lazily from chimneys and drift across the red roofs of houses. Through a telescope one can pick up lorries speeding along roads and trains steaming in and out of cuttings. Throughout the day we search hollows and woods for the flash of guns, taking bearings to them when they have been found. Early morning is the time to spot infantry movement. The men approach out of the distance in twos and threes. They may be carrying-parties or they may be runners.

By careful watching you get to know their routes and even the places to which they are going. You telephone back the target to the guns and keep them "standing to" until your victims have reached a favourable point, then you send back the order for one gun to fire. You observe where the shell lands, send back a rapid correction and, when you've got the correct line and range, bring all your guns to bear upon the target, adjusting the range and line of your shots as they run. In the dull round of an observing officer's life these little spells of manhunting are the chief excitement. There is another, however— when the enemy has spotted you and sets to work to knock you out. Neither of these diversions is likely to happen for some time yet; it's too early. Long scarves of mist are swaying low along the ground. The more distant landscape is a sea of vaporous billows, above which only the blackened fangs of trees show up.

One day the greatest excitement of all may happen: camouflaged in a pit to my right we have an anti-tank gun; in the dugout below me I have a specially selected detachment of gunners. Should the Hun make up his mind to break through, he would certainly employ tanks—perhaps some of our own, which he captured further south. Any one of these fine mornings when night is melting into dawn, our great chance may come. Then our gallant little thirteen-pounder, which has held its tongue ever since we dropped it in the trench, will start talking and we shall have a merry time, taking pot-shots over open sights, till the enemy is beaten back or we are all dead.

How many days, weeks, months have I sat here gazing on this same stretch of country? I know it all by heart—every blasted tree, every torn roadway, every ruined house. We have names for everything—Dick House, Telephone House, Lone Tree; all the names are set down on our maps. Through summer, winter and spring, ever since we first stormed the ridge, we have watched the same scene till our eyes ache with the monotony—and now again it is summer. Every now and then they have withdrawn us to put on an attack in a new part of the line, but always they have had to bring us back.

This ridge is the Gibraltar of the entire front from Ypres to Amiens; if the British were thrown back from here it would mean a huge retreat to the north and south. The Hun knows that. Directly we march out and another corps takes over from us, he begins to make his plans for an offensive. In the spring, when we were away, he put on an attack and gained a danger-ously large amount of ground. As soon as we reappeared he fell back. He has learnt the cost of provoking the Canadians—the white Gurkhas as he has called us—and prefers to express his high spirits elsewhere. So here we sit guarding our fortress, with orders to hold it at any price. The most we can do is to annoy the Hun when we're itching to crush him.

Each day we hope that our turn has come. The line is being pressed back to the south of us. Amiens and Rheims are threat-ened. Big Bertha is shelling Paris. Our nurses near the coast are being murdered by airmen. We hear of whole divisions being wiped out—of both the attacking and the attacked being so spent with fighting that they cannot raise their rifles, and crawl towards each other only to find that they have no strength in their hands to strangle. And here we sit watching, always watch-ing. It is because we are so fed up that we send out raiding par-ties. The damage they do doesn't count for much when com-pared with the total damage that the enemy is doing to us; but it's consoling. It's our way of saying, "You think you're top-dog; but the Canadians are here with their tails up. You haven't finished with the British yet—not by a damned sight."

The enemy settled his account with some of our boys last night. It appears that our party got safely to their rendezvous in No Man's Land, where they had to lie in hiding in shell-holes till the artillery started. Everything was going well and it was only a few seconds to zero hour when a returning enemy patrol stumbled across them. Our chaps didn't dare to shoot lest they should warn the garrison in the Hun front-line. They had to use their bayonets, trip them up and choke them into silence. While this was in the doing our barrage came down and then, since noise no longer mattered, they made short work of the patrol.

In this preliminary scrap Silborrad, the scout-officer, was killed. He was hugely popular with his men, for he had a reputation of always recovering his wounded. His death made them see red. When our barrage lifted and they stormed the Hun trench, they killed everything in sight; it was only when nothing living was left that they remembered that they had taken no prisoners. The proper thing to have done would have been to have come back. Their orders were not to remain in enemy territory longer than fifteen minutes; there's always the danger that the enemy supports may move up for a counter-attack and his artillery is almost certain to place a wall of fire in No Man's Land to prevent the raiders from getting back. It was Battling Brown who decided the question. "We'll take a chance at their second-line," he said. "If we don't find anyone there, we'll poke about in their communication-trenches till we do find someone."

They found the second-line strongly held by machine-gunners. There was bloody work, but they secured their prisoners. The problem now was how to get back with their dead and wounded. The green lights which the men in our front-line were shooting up to guide them, showed very faintly and were often lost to sight on account of the rolling nature of the country. The return journey was made still more difficult by snipers who picked them off as they retired. They had already entered our wire, when word was passed along that one of our men was missing. Dick must have heard it; when they were safe in our trench and called the roll, it was discovered that he too was absent. This much I learnt in the early hours from the wounded who limped up the sunken road to my left. It wasn't until dawn that I heard the rest of the story: that was when they were bringing out the dead. The engine of the ambulance had quickened its beat, getting ready to climb the hill. I ran out and found them lifting something wrapped in a blanket.

"'E was some man," one of the bearers was saying; "but 'e's too 'eavy. They 'adn't ought to 'ave brought 'im out."

Then I caught sight of Dick's gray hair. Beneath his half-shut lids his eyes still seemed to twinkle, mocking at anything good that might be said about him.

They told how, when within reach of safety, he had gone back to find the missing man. He had been gone two hours, when something was seen moving behind our wire. Just as they challenged, they recognized him by his great height. He was half-carrying, half-dragging the missing chap who had lost his way through being blinded in the encounter with the patrol. They went out to help him in with his burden. When they got to him, he said, "Boys, I'm done." After he'd spoken he just crumpled up. Blood was trickling from his mouth and, when they unbuttoned his tunic, it was sticky. Before they could bind him, he pegged out.

As I gazed down at him in the early morning twilight I could guess exactly what had happened—just as surely as if his lips had moved to tell me: he had been frightened to go back, so he went. He had wanted to go straight for her. Because he'd feared that his loneliness might trap him into beastliness, he'd come back six days ahead of time to meet his death. I wonder how much she'll care. Out here one continually wonders that about the women men spend their hearts on, idealizing them into an impossible perfection. Would she have turned her pretty back on him if he had lived to meet her? No matter, Dick; to have gone straight, even for the sake of a delusion, was worthwhile.

CHAPTER 3

During Leave

This is the kind of morning that reminds one of England; the larks are singing above the melting mists and there's a sense of peace in the air. One by one the signallers tumble up the dugout stairs; they stand in the trench yawning, stretching themselves and breathing in the golden coolness. Very lazily they set to work preparing breakfast. They have to be careful lest any smoke escapes and gives away our post to the enemy. If once the Hun suspected we were here, it wouldn't take him long to knock us out. They'll be bringing me in some stewed tea presently; I can hear the bacon sizzling. I wish there was some water to wash with; but we gave most of ours to the wounded last night.

I was in England this spring when the big Hun drive against Paris started. I'd just recovered from being wounded and directly I heard the news, commenced moving heaven and earth to get back. Heaven and earth didn't require much moving—men were too badly needed. I reported back to my reserve depot on a Wednesday and within the hour was told that I could proceed on the next draft leaving for France. I was given a two days' leave to collect my kit, and permission to join the draft at the London station.

That London leave is curiously blurred in my memory. It was only my body that was in England; my soul was in France. I rushed from tailors to bankers, from bankers to boot-makers, from boot-makers to lunches and theatres; I met people and laughed with people and said "Goodbye" to people, but there was nothing real in anything that I saw or did. In imagination I saw myself on the Amiens road fighting.

"Our backs are to the wall," Sir Douglas Haig had told us. "The Canadians will advance or fall with their faces to the foe"—that was how my corps commander's special order had run. Every moment that I was not there with the chaps seemed shameful. If we were beaten back it seemed that it would be my fault—one more man in the line might make all the difference.

How little I was noticing the world about me was emphasized by one small incident. I had been taxi-riding all over the map in a frenzied effort to collect my gear. In these war-days London taxi-drivers have developed short tempers, especially for fares who keep them waiting. My man had been extraordinarily docile. At the end of two hours, when I had deposited some of my baggage at Victoria, I said to him, "I suppose I'd better pay you off now. I've got to go to Battersea; you won't want to go there, so I'll have to go by train."

"My time's yours," said the man. "We can't get any jobs since this offensive started; all the officers have left for France."

It was true, and I hadn't noticed it. The restaurants were empty, except for a few civilians. You could get seats for any theatre and as many as you wanted. Almost overnight the soldier-men had departed.

I remember with peculiar vividness the attitude of my friends towards me. They treated me as a person who tomorrow would be dead—the way we treated men in khaki in 1914, before we had learnt that not every man who goes into battle stays there a corpse. My two brothers got leave from the Navy and came to see me off. I left them to do the booking of rooms at the hotel: when we went up to bed the night before I started, I found that instead of booking three rooms, they had booked one room with two beds. I didn't comment on it.

It was dark when we rose. While we dressed, we talked emptily with a feverish jocularity. In the midst of a hurried breakfast four friends appeared, who had given me no previous warning of their intentions. They were people who liked their comfort; they must have travelled by workmen's trains to get there. Chatting with a spurious gaiety, we walked over to the station through the damp raw half-light. I wasn't allowed to carry anything. As though their minds were clocks ticking, I could hear them repeating over and over, "The Canadians will advance, or fall with their faces to the foe. Our backs are to the wall—He'll fall," they kept repeating; "he'll fall."

The platform was dense with khaki. Here and there one saw a frail old lady seeing her son off; there was a sprinkling of girls, who clung to their men's arms and made a brave attempt to laugh. Then, before anything sincere had been done or said, everyone was taking his seat and the doors were being locked. There was no khaki on the platform now—only the drab of civilian costume, which made its wearers look like mourners. I leant out of the window. Suddenly one of my women friends, who had never done such a thing before, drew herself up by my hand and kissed me. The wheels began to revolve.

"When you get there, keep your heads down," the men on the platform called.

"Cheerio, old things," we answered.

The girls tried to say something, put their hands to their throats and choked. Their smiles became masks. Then we were out of the station, speeding past housetops, with the wheels singing triumphantly, "The Canadians will advance—advance—advance."

We were all Canadians in my carriage. We had all been wounded—some once, some oftener. "Well, we can't get there too soon," one said. To parade our assumed indifference, we began to play cards. Farther down the train, above the roar of our going, we could hear the cheery voices of the "other ranks" singing, *"Good-bye-ee Don't cry-ee Wipe the tear, baby dear, from your eye-ee."*

We were trying to bluff it out to all the sleeping country that we didn't care and rather liked dying.

The base-port across the Channel at which we landed was in strange contrast to London's haggard smiling. It not only did not care, but it totally ignored the fact that "our backs were to the wall." Nothing had changed since we had seen it last. People were no cheerier, no duller. They had the same bored air of carrying on with what they obviously regarded as "a hell of a job."

The dugout colonels and majors, who handed us our transportation, were just as fussily convinced as ever that they alone were conducting the war. On the journey up the line the only signs of menace were trench-systems hastily thrown up far back of where any had been before, a rather unusual amount of new ordnance on trucks and the greater frequence of hospital trains, hurrying towards the Channel. The idea that we were soon to be corpses began to fade; we played cards more assiduously that we might keep normal. Now and then, as we passed towns, we looked out of the window. We began to recognise the names of stations and to guess at the part of the front to which we were going. We ceased guessing; we knew at last.

"So he's attacking the Vimy Ridge," we thought.

It was a year since our corps had captured it: if the capturing of it had been a bloody affair, the defending of it against overwhelming odds would be twice as bloody. In imagination I could smell the horror of the unburied dead of Farbus and see the galloping of the shells, like the hoofs of invisible cavalry, up the road from Willerval. The fallen victors of last year's fight would be stirring in their shallow graves and pushing their bones above the ground in protest.

All this I saw as I journeyed and played cards. And when I got here I found that it was to this I was returning—to this intolerable inertia of watching. "The Canadians will advance or fall with their faces to the foe." Brave words! But we have neither advanced, nor fallen. In utter weariness, but with purpose unbroken, other men are crawling into battle on their hands and knees before Amiens, while we sit still, with the indignity of not dying upon us.

CHAPTER 4

Two New Volunteers

The major has just phoned me to say that there's an officer coming forward to relieve me, and that he won't be one of us. That sets me wondering; does it mean that we're going to be pulled out to take part in the fight? There have been all kinds of rumours going the rounds this summer—rumours to the effect that when Foch has let the Hun advance far enough our corps is to be made the hammer-head of the offensive which is to push him back. There would seem to be some truth in the report, for every time we've been withdrawn from the line it's been to practise open warfare. We've rehearsed with tanks and aeroplanes, and fought sham battles in which nearly all our work has consisted in coming into action at the gallop. We've been nicknamed "Foch's Pets," which may not mean very much; but it at least seems certain that when the Allies' drive starts we shall be in it. The thought is intoxicating: it means the end of waiting.

But what will become of Bully Beef and his mother if we sail off into the blue on a great attack? Bully Beef and his mother need explaining; they have no official standing—they are members of our battery whom the army does not recognize. Bully Beef is a little boy in skirts, about four years old I should hazard. His mother is a French girl of not more than twenty; she is not married.

Bully Beef introduced himself to the battery about two months ago when we were out at training. He used to hide himself in the hedge of a deeply wooded lane which climbed the hill to the sergeants' mess; from this point of vantage he used to throw sticks and stones at anyone in khaki. He had long hair down to the middle of his small fat back; this, taken in conjunction with his skirts, left all the battery fully persuaded for a week that he was a girl. On account of his supposed sex he was not chastised for his stone-throwing. We called him "Little Sister."

Our wagon-lines lay at the bottom of the hill in a meadow the length of which a tiny river ran. Along the sides of the river bushes grew in tangled profusion. It was here that we held our watering parades, leading our horses close to the edge of the bank so that they could dip their noses in the ripples. In the woods near by our men had their bivouacs, creating the appearance of a gipsy-camp.

At the top of the meadow our guns and wagons were parked; behind them in three straight lines our horses had their standings. In the bowl of the valley, as far as eye could stretch, the wheat grew yellow. Round the lip of the bowl, where the hills touched the sky, the coolness of woods drew a thick green line. It was a very quiet spot, mellow with nightingales, and lazy with summer. It gave no hint of battle, except at night when the bombing planes came over to destroy us and the chalky fingers of searchlights unravelled the clouds and suddenly pointed. When they pointed, every Archie for miles round would open up at an intense rate of fire.

I say it gave no hint of battle. That is not quite precise. What I mean is that the country itself gave no hint of unrest in its own appearance. Among the people the signs were plentiful. There were ourselves for instance. Every village was packed with storm-troops, being fattened up like turkeys for killing. There were Chinamen building new railways through the grain in preparation for the retreat which seemed inevitable. All kinds of new trench-systems were being dug, that we might dispute every inch of territory. Down the gleaming roads little processions of refugees were continually passing, led by an old horse, tied together with rope and string, and harnessed into a creaking dilapidated wagon.

The wagon was invariably overloaded with things which

looked absolutely worthless. On the shafts of the wagon a disconsolate man would sit, staring vacantly at everything and nothing. Following behind on foot would come a dog, some dirty children and a draggle-tailed woman. The woman seemed to be the least important part of the man's possessions. Only the mouldy skeleton between the shafts seemed to hold any place in his affections; it helped him to escape. Every day such processions crawled through the sunshine. Our men laughed and shared their rations with the children. Ah, how merry we were and how much we laughed while we waited for death to call us! The refugees were fleeing towards life—a life which they dreaded. We had nothing to fear from living—life had done its worst.

Not for an hour in the day or night did the guns cease their distant chiding, lowing like cattle and bidding us return. That we would return dramatically and without warning we were well aware. We were only ignorant of the place and time. We had cut down our kits to what was absolutely necessary; everything superfluous had been returned to Blighty. Our brigade held itself in readiness to march at a two hours' notice. Most significant of all, every day both officers and men spent hours at the ranges, learning to be marksmen. This in itself was prophetic of close and desperate fighting—it meant that the enemy was expected to be up against the muzzles of our guns. Who ever dreamt until now of training artillery to be riflemen!

These were the conditions under which we made Bully Beef's acquaintance. The sergeants' mess was in the cottage where his mother lived; he soon made friends with the sergeant-major. It wasn't long before he began to appear upon parades, his grubby hand held fast in the big brown fist of one of the drivers or gunners. It was bad for good order and discipline, but none of us officers had the heart to forbid him. He soon learnt to obey the orders "Shun" and "Stand at ease," and would hold himself steady with "eyes front" to be inspected. It was about a fortnight after we had been billeted in the village that we discovered that we could no longer call him "Little Sister": he fell into the river when the horses were watering and had to go naked while his clothes were drying.

His parentage was a problem. Some said that he was the child of a rich married Frenchman; others that his father had been a quartermaster in a Highland battalion. We rather clung to the legend of his Scotch origin; his sturdy habit of throwing stones at people bigger than himself seemed to prove that he was British.

His mother is difficult to describe. She's a pleasant, sun-browned girl, with a happy smile and kindly ways of showing her contentment. She rarely looks at you; her eyes, which are gray, are always demurely cast down, and yet you feel that all the time she's watching. Her head is always bare so that her hair, which would naturally be brown, is bleached to the colour of honey. Whenever you pass her she is humming a little song, and sometimes she laughs beneath her breath. Her hands are interminably busy, doing something for Bully Beef or some of our men. She devours her little son with a hungry passion and pushes him away from her in pretence that she does not care. Everything that she does she clothes in an atmosphere of tenderness. What her name is none of us know for certain, but we call her Suzette.

When we received the order to march out from her village, we thought that we were going into an attack, instead of which at the end of the long night march we found ourselves again on the Ridge. Because it was night when we moved, nobody noticed that Suzette was following. I don't believe she walked; I suspect that she rode in a G. S. wagon with the connivance of the captain and the quartermaster-sergeant. When we found her at our new wagon-lines in the morning, no one felt like reporting officially on her presence.

Since then she has made herself the mother of our battery; it's to Suzette that we all go when we've lost a button or our clothes need patching. And it's to Suzette that we go when the letters from our girls aren't up to scratch. We just sit a little while and look at her; after that we renew our faith in women and feel better.

The men have built her a little bivouac a short distance away from theirs, yet within ear-range if she should need them. Woe betide any blackguard who tries to molest her. It's happened twice; the men lay cold for the best part of an hour. They were strangers from another unit.

How does she exist on active service? The cook feeds her on the sly from the battery-kitchen. The men share with her the boxes that are sent to them from home. Our first thought on looking through a present of comforts is, "Ah, that will do for Suzette." For the rest, the quartermaster supplies her with necessities and blankets. Of late she has taken to wearing a Tommy's tunic and a khaki shirt.

Suzette has become an institution; the colonel and general are aware of her; they both wink at her presence. They may well, for she keeps our men straight; there's been no drunkenness since she came among us. She'll be the last woman to be seen by many of our chaps; the casualties in our counter-offensive are bound to be heavy.

What I'm wondering is will she be allowed to accompany us if we go into open warfare; we can scarcely have a woman with us then. I'd bet the shirt off my back, however, that the captain will manage it. He never speaks to her or of her—never seems to notice her; but if you watch him closely, you know that he listens for her laughter and her footstep. He's a man to whom something shattering has happened—something not done by shells. He was badly wounded last year at Vimy; we none of us expected to see him back. He rejoined us suddenly in the spring. He's come back to die; we all know that. By this time next year, if he can contrive it bravely, he won't be listening for Suzette or any girl.

CHAPTER 5

Marsh Valley

The officer who's going to relieve me has just arrived and gone forward to battalion headquarters with one of my linesmen. He's poking round the front just at present; as soon as he comes back, he'll take over from me and I shall report to my major at the guns.

Queer, the places men go to in this war and the circumstances under which they meet! This chap went to school with me in London, I discover. I remember him chiefly by one of those inconsequential incidents of childhood; he had a hoydenish sister who laid me out by throwing a snowball with a stone in it. She's a married woman with children now—the wife of one of the props of the upper middle-classes. Her husband has a seat in Parliament; before the war she owned a Rolls Royce and everything else that was respectable. She's been going up in the social scale ever since she threw that snowball. It's by the snowball that she recalls me, her brother tells me, whenever my name is mentioned.

This chap's been to the east; he was present at the taking of Bagdad. He speaks of all that magic country as though it were just as commonplace as this desolate plain of ruined villages on which I gaze.

Tonight we pull our guns out. Where we're going nobody knows. Our infantry are already marching out in sections and the Imperials are taking over from us. Staff officers with their red tabs go up and down the trenches. Brass-hats pass down the sunken road and pop their heads in at my observation post to enquire their direction. There's mystery and excitement in the air. They can't be withdrawing us for a third time merely to go into training. It must be for the counter-stroke which we have so long expected. But when are we going to strike and where?

I'd like to see our captain at this moment. The whole impatience of our corps through this summer seems to be summed up in his person. Like all of us, only more so, he has listened since the spring with a kind of agony for the galloping of the black horseman who rides alone. He himself is a man who rides solitarily. His eyes have a steady forward gaze, quiet and firm and unflinching. I shouldn't say he was a good soldier—not in details or in the ordinary sense; he came into the war, as most of us did, too late in life for that. In peace times he was a painter and a *dilettante*, noted for many oddities which do not matter now. He was successful and courted and on the crest of the wave. When war broke out, he downed tools at once and offered himself for cannon-fodder.

In August 1914 a new way of valuing men came into fashion. Death is the sincerest of all democrats. It did not matter who we were, what our attainments, wealth, position: the chimney-sweep and the genius were of equal worth. Kreisler's bow-arm was only of service to his country for firing a rifle. A man might have the greatest singing voice in Europe; his voice would not help. We required of him his body; it would stop a bullet. When we reached the trenches, we learnt even more dramatically that nothing that we had been counted. Only the heart that was in us could raise us above our fellows—or to use the more colloquial army term, "the guts."

Guts would enable a man to fight on when hope had retreated, until hope in very shame returned. A man who hadn't guts was shot at the back of the line by his comrades as a deserter. A man who had was shot up front as a white man with his face towards the enemy. There was no appeal from these alternatives; birth, talents, money could not disturb the sentence. There was only one standard by which our worth was estimated—the measure of our sacrificial courage.

Of course we were all inefficient. We had never dreamt of being soldiers till the deluge of brutality poured out of Germany and threatened to destroy the world. We were specialists in various small departments of human knowledge; our special knowledge, unless it was military, was no longer of service. That was the hard part of it—that many of us who had known the pride of being specialists, were now called upon to approve ourselves in an effort for which we were totally unfitted. Of all the qualities which we had cultivated so carefully the world asked for the one to which we had paid least attention—our courage. So the captain laid down his brush, turned his canvases to the wall, joined as an artillery driver and went to grooming horses.

When his training was ended and he was shot out to the front, he learnt almost overnight the tremendous lesson that it's the spirit that counts—the thing that a man is essentially inside himself and not the thing which his social advantages make him appear to other people. A man cannot camouflage under shellfire; in the face of death his true worth becomes known to everybody. When war started, judgement day commenced in the world for every man who put on khaki. God estimated us in the front-line, and God's eyes were the eyes of our fellows.

I believe the captain had expected that he would prove himself a coward—most of us expected that for ourselves. When he found that he could be fearless, the relief was so triumphant that he became possessed by an immense elation. He took the wildest chances and was always trying to outdo in heroism his own last bravest act. Promotion came rapidly; at the end of eight months he was a sergeant and before the year was out had gained his commission.

He joined our brigade as an officer in September of 1916, when we were waiting on the high ground behind Albert, preparatory to being flung into the cauldron of the Somme offensive. He was treated with suspicion at first; no one expected much from a chap who had been a painter. The colonel sniffed contemptuously when he reported at the tent which was brigade headquarters.

"What were you before you became a soldier?"

"A painter, sir."

"Of houses?"

"No. Of landscapes and portraits."

To a hustler who has flung railroads across continents, outwitting nature and abbreviating time, to have been a painter seemed a sorry occupation—an occupation which indicated long hair, innumerable cigarettes, artists' models and silken ways of life. The colonel himself had been in the North-West Mounted Police and had lived furiously, tracking outlaws and rounding up Indians.

"So you've been a painter, Heming," he sniffed. "Out here we don't do much that's in your line. We deal in only two colours: the mud-brown of weariness and the scarlet of sacrifice. We don't copy landscapes—we make them."

Heming was attached to a battery whose major was noted for his "guts." He either made or broke his officers in the first week that they were with him. He didn't have to wait long to be put to the test. The whole of our brigade was crowded into the narrow valley, know as Mash Valley, which parallels the road which runs along the ridge from Albert to Pozieres. It was a direct enfilade for the Hun. The batteries were strung throughout the length of the valley at about two-hundred-yard intervals, so that when we weren't being pounded by the enemy, we were being wounded by premature from the friendly guns behind us.

When a strafe was on, it was as though two contending gales had met above our heads and were pushing against each other breast to breast. In those days we made landscapes at a tremendous rate. There met at the Somme the most ingenious artists in the science of destruction which the world had seen till that date. They found a pleasant country of windmills, snuggling woods, villages with tall, clear spires, nests of embowered greenness upheld by hills against the sky, and they trampled it with shells into dust and mixed the dust with the blood of men, till as far as eye could stretch it was a putrescent sea of mud.

In the first week of September 1916, when we crept into our positions under the heavy morning mist, the clay was baked to the brittle hardness of pottery; two months earlier the rains and carnage had washed away all signs of friendliness and greenness. Hands, heads and stockinged feet of the dead stuck out where the mud had dried up; one tripped over them and, at touching them, shrank back with a thrill of horror.

It was a good place from many points of view to test a man's capacity for "guts." It was especially good at night, for directly darkness had fallen the Hun drenched the length and breadth of the valley with gas-shells You could hear them coming over with a whistling sound, like an army of wild geese. You waited for the explosions and, when you heard nothing but stealthy thuds, you knew that it was time to run along the gun-pits and give the alarm for the wearing of gas-helmets.

The helmets with which we were issued in those days were rather horrid affairs. They were like gray flannel shirts drenched in treacle and sewn up at the top so that you could not push your head through. You pulled them on and tucked the shirts in under the collar of your tunic. Then you shoved a rubber mouth-piece between your teeth, peered out through the goggles in the side of the gray flannel and slowly suffocated. Seeing that we were in a valley, all the gas from the shells drifted down to the low ground where the gun-pits had been dug and hung there ready to stifle your men directly the suffocation of their helmets became too much to bear. Mash Valley was most excellently chosen as a place in which to test one's guts.

Heming had been with us two days when the major took him up with him to make a reconnaissance of the front. At that time I was corporal of the B. C. party, so I went ahead to lay in wire in order that we might keep in touch with the battery should the major wish to register the guns. At the head of Mash Valley there was an engineers' dump, known as Kay, and it was at this point that the main trench-system began. We ran our wire in as far as Kay and were met there by the major and Heming at three in the morning.

A Scotch mist was drifting across the desolation. The air was piercingly cold and a watery moon looked down. I think the first thing that impressed one about the trenches of the Somme was their desertion. The dead far outnumbered the living, and the dead were for the most part unburied. One wondered from where the men would spring up to fight should a Hun attack commence. The walls of the trenches were honey-combed with little scooped out holes. In those holes, with their knees drawn up to their chins and the mist soaking down on them, unshaven haggard men slept. They were polluted to the eyes and wearied to extinction. Sometimes their feet stuck out across the duck-board. You stumbled across them, but they did not waken; they only moaned. When they did not moan, you were puzzled; until a man made some motion or spoke, you were never certain whether he was living or dead. The slain defenders and those who had taken over from them huddled side by side, keeping guard together.

Here and there one of the kennels had been crushed in by a shell and the inmate had been killed while he slept. His *putteed* legs and heavy army boots were still thrust out across the duck-board; they were the only reminders of his sojourn there.

As one drew nearer to the front-line through the winding labyrinth of trenches, he noticed that the sides were walled up with the dead. Men's bodies had proved cheaper than sandbags; moreover, they had saved labour in spots where no unnecessary men ought to be asked to jeopardize their lives. The bodies, where they showed through the mud, had flaked off white like plaster exposed to the wind and sun. Flies rose up in clouds as one passed; their wings filled the air with an incessant buzzing.

Horrors multiplied as the world grew grayer and the dawn began to break. We came to a ditch levelled nearly flat by the Hun barrage, in which Jocks and coloured troops had fought side by side. They were buried to the waist; in the process of decay the black men had turned white and the white black.

I watched the effect of all this on Heming. The major watched him. Perhaps most closely of all the signallers watched him.

When a new officer joins any unit, the men are overwhelmingly eager to find out whether he has guts. They know that the day is always coming when their chance of life may depend on his judgment and courage.

Heming's face was the face of a dreamer.—He never was nor could have been a man of action. He imagined too far ahead. He visualized and fought the horror which lurked behind each traverse before he came to it. A thousand times that morning he must have seen himself mutilated and dead. His expression was tense and excited, but an amused smile played about the edges of his mouth. His eyes beneath his steel-helmet were brilliant and forward-looking. He seemed to contemplate his inward struggle against terror with the unimpassioned aloofness of a spectator.

Trenches were becoming shallower. It was some time since we had passed any sentries or working-parties. A horrible, brooding silence was over everything, broken only by the secret dripping of rain and the scuttling of rats among corpses. The major became more frequent in the examining of his map. At last he ordered us to crouch down while he stealthily peered over the lip of the trench in an effort to get his bearings. It began to dawn on us that we had come too far and were lost in No Man's Land.

While we waited, behind the mist we heard talking. The mist parted and we saw, not fifty yards away, the smoke-gray uniforms and red-cross armlets of a party of Hun stretcher-bearers. The major was standing up. The Huns dropped the stretcher they were carrying; at the same instant a rifle rang out. The major toppled backward, tearing at his breast.

Then we learnt once and for all whether Heming had guts. His face leapt together—these are the only words in which to describe his sudden change of expression. The entire man became knit in one purpose, to out-daunt the challenge of the danger. His eyes were merry when he turned to me. "There are just enough of you to carry the major out. He may live if you get him to a dressing-station. Work your way back down this trench; you'll strike our front-line somewhere in that direction."

"But what about you, sir?" I asked.

He was examining his revolver to see whether it was clean and ready. "I'm going forward," he answered. "If I can get in a few pot-shots, I'll divert their attention and help you to make good your getaway."

It was the damnedest bit of folly—one man with a revolver, going forward to stir up an unknown number of the enemy. He was an officer, so we had to obey him; besides, there were only just enough of us to carry out the major. Just as we had started, Heming came crawling back to me on his hands and knees.

"Corporal," he said hurriedly, "if anything should happen to me, just drop a line to this address and let her know that I wasn't yellow. I don't suppose she'll care, so you don't need to be sentimental. Just state the fact, and say that I did everything that she might feel proud of—of our friendship."

The address which he slipped into my hand bore the name of a married woman. I recognized her name, for I had seen her portrait often in the *London Illustrateds*. I wondered whether it was true what he had said, that she would not care.

There wasn't much time for wondering; the mist was lifting. It was easy to see one's direction now and easy to be seen by the enemy. The trench was shallow; it was exhausting work, crouching to take advantage of every bit of cover and dragging at the body of the wounded man. We hadn't been gone ten minutes before a barrage came down on the spot where we had been discovered, setting up a wall of fire between ourselves and Heming. In the brief silences between the falling of the shells, I could hear the ping of rifle-bullets. They were passing far over to our left; I could picture how Heming was exposing himself to draw the fire away from us.

It took us two hours to get the major back to our lines. The last part of the way we grew reckless and carried him overland. Our infantry saw us and came out with a stretcher to help. At the dressing-station the M. O who attended to the wound broke the news abruptly, "He hasn't an earthly."

The major's eyes opened. He repeated the words, "Not an earthly." And then, "Tell Heming he's all right, and say—say I'm sorry I doubted."

The major went west one hour after that and we returned to the guns to report to Brigade what had happened. The report went in across the wire, but the colonel at once sent for me to give him the details in person. When I had ended, he sat twisting his moustaches thoughtfully.

Then, "That fool painter," he said, talking more to himself than to me, "I suppose he knew I thought he was afraid."

And then to me, "But he's all white, corporal, and it's up to us to get him out. D'you think you could find the way back?"

I told him I could by following the wire which we had laid to that point.

When we again reached Kay Dump and Tom's Cut, which was the main trench leading to the frontline, we found that the usual morning "hate" was in progress. The wounded of the night before were being carried out; as the bearers, carrying the stretchers on their shoulders, reached the high ground, the Huns caught sight of them and started to mow them down with enfilade fire. Our guns opened up in retaliation; by the time the strafe had died down the morning had become too clear for anyone to approach No Man's Land without being observed. It was in the first dusk of evening that Heming came back. We were in the front-line waiting for him, when the Hun snipers opened up. We saw him come running in zig-zags through the rusty wire and shell-holes. When he jumped into the trench beside us, he was laughing. "I've had a simply ripping time, Corporal," he commenced.

Then, seeing the colonel, he stood stiffly to attention and saluted.

"What doing?" the colonel asked.

"Making landscapes," said Heming, with a twinkle, "and letting daylight into Huns."

So that was how our captain proved that he had guts; he's done nothing but add to the reputation which he then earned. It was on the way down to the battery that he asked me to give him back the address. "And you must never mention her name, corporal. Promise me that."

Today I am an officer with Heming in the same battery, and we have never referred to the matter. I am sure he is in love with her and I believe he was in love with her before she married. Why he missed her or what are their present relations, I cannot guess; all I know is that he is out here to die and that she is the inspiration of all his reckless courage. Now he knows that the counter-stroke is to be struck and that the big chance of death has come, his heart will be singing. The men as they go about their packing up will be following him with their eyes and whispering, "The Captain's mighty cheerio. He's all for it." In watching him they will feel a thrill of excitement; they, too, will become "all for it." They will go with him anywhere—if need be, to hell.

Mighty cheerio and all for it! That's the way the entire Canadian Corps must be feeling at this moment. All through the sunny days of spring and summer we have had to sit tight and watch while other men marched out to meet their death. Thank God, our turn to sacrifice has come. The indignity of not dying is at last removed from us.

Chapter 6

New Orders

It was growing dusk before the observing-officer of the re-lieving battery returned from his reconnaissance of the front to take over from me. The Hun planes had already come out like monstrous bats from their hiding-places, and were dipping their wings in the aquamarine and saffron of the fading sky. Our ma-chine-gunners and riflemen for miles round were busy taking pot-shots at them, trying to drive them back so that they should not detect the unusual movement of troops behind our lines.

One may say what he likes about war, but it has moments which possess a surpassing and enthralling beauty. One such moment came this evening as I watched what is likely to prove to be my last sunset over the Vimy plain. I know it all—every charred tree, every hollow, every shattered ruin. I ought to know it for it has made me suffer; Death, mounted on his black stal-lion, has waited for me behind almost every bit of cover within sight. I have felt him when I could not see him; there have been times when across the distance I have caught the gleam of his shrouded eyes.

Because of these things, because of the friends who have died here, because of the risks we have taken and shared, because of the ice-cold nights, the poker-games, the brief escapes into cleaner country, the letters from a certain girl and the home-sick dreams which have wiled away tedious hours in dug-outs— because of all these things, in an obstinate kind of way I love the scarred, forsaken horror of this country. "For the last time," I told myself as I watched the sunset glow grow fainter upon the enemy domes and spires of Douai.

If I live through the war I may come back to this ridge which has been my home for over a year; but, if I come back, it will not look the same. All the challenge to one's daring will have vanished. There will be no gassing, no shelling; one will be able to expose himself as much as he likes. Everything will be desperately and conventionally safe. Curious how one learns to admire danger!

While I watched and the light faded, men became symbols and shadows. They crept along the trenches, going up to die, as men have gone up to die through the ages. Even in peace times we were soldiers for one cause or another, and none of us were immune from dying. We are fighting from the day we draw breath till the day when our bodies, like beggars' rags, drop from us and our spirits in their swift lean whiteness escape. Death! What is it but just that, the casting aside of tattered clothing!— and how tattered one's body can become in the front-line!

The dance of destruction commenced as darkness settled. Like ropes of pearls flung up, the luminous tracer-bullets of machine-guns darted towards the sky. From somewhere in the clouds the Hun planes replied, flinging down similar ropes of ruin. Against the horizon, like lilies floating, Hun flares soared and swayed. While they lasted, Gavrelle sprang ghostly into sight and the contorted skeleton of what once was Oppy. The flares sink and die, everything is again swallowed up in obscurity. Down the sunken road to my left go the anonymous feet of marching men. Other feet have trampled that mud, and they now are silent. There are feet among those who march tonight which will not make the return journey.

The phone rings sharply. "You're wanted, sir." The message is shouted up from the depths of the dugout. I press the button of my flash-lamp and hurriedly slither down the innumerable greasy stairs. As I take the receiver, I tell the signaller to light another candle as there may be a message to pencil. He lights the candle and sticks it against the planked wall in the orthodox way, by warming the wall with the flame so that the heat may melt the wax.

"Hulloa! Hulloa! Oh, it's you sir!" It's my major. "No, the friend who came to see me this morning has not returned; he went somewhere. Yes, I know; he ought to have taken over from me. O, here he is. You'll have horses for all my party. Yes, sir, I understand. I won't waste any time."

I turn round to the officer who is to relieve me. "You took your time, old thing, I must say. I hope the dinner at battalion headquarters was a wet one. But you've rather crowded me; my battery hits the trail tonight."

He starts a lengthy explanation, but I'm in a hurry to be gone. While I hand over to him my fighting maps, my linesmen are loading themselves with reels of wire and instruments.

"Well, so long," I say.

"Good luck," he replies.

How often I have spoken such words in this cramped death-trap; now I'm speaking them for the last time. I take a final look round; there's the frame-work bunk, with the chicken-wire nailed over it, on which I have spent so many restless nights; there's the ground-sheet tacked over the second exit through which the draught was so persistent in coming; there's the pencilled message on the wall to his sweetheart in the Argonne from the captured French soldier who slaved for the Hun—a message of deathless love, which I forwarded to her as directed. This place was a home of sorts, and now it is another's.

We scramble up the steep, clammy stairs into the trench. The night air is soft and warm; stars are coming out. Round the traverse where the thirteen-pounder lies concealed, the gun-detachment is waiting for me. I raise the camouflage to take one last look at the brave little piece; then I'm tempted to enter and to place my hand upon the smooth cold breech-block, which shines like silver.

"We never got our chance to fire you, old girl," is my thought; "but we'd have done our bit, if the Hun tanks had come, you and I. If the chance does come, you'll have to play the game with some other chap now."

We're in the sunken road, climbing the ridge where the chalk gleams white as snow in the darkness. Some runners go past us, smoking cigarettes. They belong to the relieving troops; none of our men would do that. A cigarette shows up like a lamp from this point of vantage. I halt the men and order them to put out their cigarettes.

We're on the crest now, where a sentry challenges. To the right and left shells are falling with a sullen crash. Our faces are turned towards the west, where the horizon is still faintly flame-coloured and evening has not yet sunk into night. To our right the splinted tower of Mount St. Eloi points a martyred finger at the clouds. Beneath our feet runs the Concrete Road, built at such sacrifice across the torn battlefield. All our transport comes up along this route, as the Hun knows well; he makes it the special target of his harassing fire.

We note the new hits which the enemy has scored on it since last we made the journey. The ground is ploughed with shells on either side; here and there one finds black pools of blood, dead horses and broken limbers. From craters and places of conceal-ment our forward guns belch fire. Their flash is hidden from the enemy by the ridge; but he has guessed their approximate loca-tions, and searches and sweeps day and night in an effort to find and destroy them. Now and then, like the blast of a furnace, a torrent of flame shoots up where he has exploded an ammuni-tion dump. Against the swift and momentary illumination one sees the shadowy figures of men running and dropping into shell-holes. The spectacle of death fails to move us. We have be-come too used to dying.

As we plod along under our heavy loads of instruments, kit, revolvers and reels of wire, we spread out so that one shell may not get the lot of us. My men are singing; from the words I gather an idea of what is happening in their minds:

I said "Goodbye" to the flowers
And "Goodbye" to the trees,
And the little church which sleeps so quietly,

I said "Goodbye" to on my knees;
I said "Goodbye" to my sister
And my dear old mammy, too;
But my heart was almost breaking
When I said "Goodbye" to you.

They're conscious of something different and devastating approaching, and are singing their farewell to security.

Foch's Pets! The hammer-head of the counterattack! If that's the game, there won't be many of us left to celebrate peace. It's August now; how many of us will be above ground by Christmas?

Chapter 7

Secret Orders

We found our horses waiting for us with the grooms and horse-holders in a trench about fifty yards off the road. They had had to take cover there on account of enemy shelling attracted by an anti-aircraft battery. The anti-aircraft battery being mounted on motor-lorries, had made a swift get-away the moment the retaliation, which they had called down, had started. Our boys couldn't get away; they had received explicit orders to wait for me and my party with their horses at one specific point on the Concrete Road. Three horses had been slightly wounded and one of the men had been killed. A splinter of shell had cut his throat as completely as if a knife had been drawn across it.

Kneeling beside the body, I drew back the saddle-blanket which had been thrown over it and scanned the face with my flash-lamp. My groom touched me on the shoulder, "You won't recognise him, sir; he's a remount—only came to the front for the first time yesterday evening."

It was a young face, with scarcely any beard on it. Nineteen, at most. The eyes were blue, and filmed, and wide. They had a sudden expression of surprise and protest. Death doesn't often disturb me now-a-days, but I couldn't bear that scarlet mark across the throat.—One day at the wagon-lines, being chaffed for having come into the army late—the next night dead! Poor laddie! I don't know who you are or where you came from. If I could have prevented it, things shouldn't have happened this way. They ought to have given you a better run for your money.

I'm sorry.

The horses are snorting and jumping back against the reins, so I switch off my flashlight and cover up the face.

"Have any arrangements been made?" I ask.

They tell me "None"—the accident only happened within the last half-hour.

"Then one of you will have to mount it in front of you. Hand it over to the captain of the relieving battery. He'll have to see to its burial; we march within the next three hours. Where's the major?"

I learn that he's still at the guns, so I tell my groom to lead on down the road to the battery-position and I order the rest of the party to get mounted. As I turn to take a short-cut through the rusty wire of old defences and the water-logged craters of unrecorded fights, I glance back to catch the silhouettes of the horsemen as they ride towards the red lip of the horizon, with the drooping body hanging sack-like in front of the last rider's saddle. An inconspicuous ending to one lad's dreams of glory! He won't be here for the counter-stroke. Letters from home will arrive full of anxiety and affection. They'll have to be returned unread and unopened. The old, sad story! And yet, who knows! Perhaps he's lucky.

Ahead of me in the misty vagueness of the chalk lies a ray of light like a golden dagger. I slide down into a trench, which was the Hun front-line. Poppies and cornflowers grow in tufts along its sides. Beneath my feet I feel the slats of duckboard. Dug back into the wall is a six-foot square room, with anti-gas blankets hung before it. The curtain which they form has not been properly adjusted; from between its edges light escapes. I lift the curtain and enter.

About a trench-made table a group of officers are seated. All of them are strangers to me except my major; they're the new chaps who are taking over from us. On the table there are two whiskey bottles, one empty and one just broached. There's a tin jug of water, a medley of glasses, piles of matches which are being used as poker-chips and a dealt-out hand of cards.

My major's face, which is usually pale, is flushed tonight. His eyes are wrinkled and red about the edges; but the eyes themselves are like two blue pools of fire. As he catches sight of me, he raises his glass, "We don't know where we're going, Chris. Everything's secret. All we know is that we march tonight and that they've got a labour battalion digging graves for us somewhere behind the line. Oh yes, and a special lorry of Victoria Crosses has arrived at corps. We're storm-troops, my boy, and going to be in it right up to the neck. Where-ever we march and whenever we fight, here's the old toast, 'Success to crime.'"

I manage to let him know that our horses are outside and hint that it's about time we were going.

"Time! There's heaps of time," he says. "We pulled our guns out early this evening. The battery is all packed and back at the wagon-lines. Heming will have it standing to when we arrive. Sit down and take a hand. God knows when we'll get a chance of a round of poker again."

My mind is not on the game. I'm losing steadily, but I don't worry. The candles drip away in wax; others take their places. I scarcely see the cards; I watch only one face through the wreaths of tobacco-smoke—my gallant little major's. I would never have known him in peace life; neither of us would have considered the other quite his sort. He looks like a cross between a clown and an ostler. He's very small and slight; his legs are bowed with too much riding. If one were to see him in civilian dress, it would seem right that he should be chewing a straw. His face is white as death and terribly worn. His hair is sandy and thin in places. His teeth are filled with chunks of gold and not very regular.

His uniforms are never smart; after he's had them a week, they're always torn and stained. He's like a bantam cock; he makes up in spirit what he misses in height. He says "Good-bye" to his temper on the first provocation and is always most handsomely sorry afterwards.   He's adored and dreaded by his men. He's the best field-gunner for open warfare in the whole Canadian Corps. His superior officers twit and admire him. He has an extraordinary talent for collaring affection. One trusts his judgment absolutely and yet follows him with a feeling that he must be protected. Life hasn't been very good to him; he's not particular as to whether or no he survives the fighting! There used to be a girl in the background—Well, there's no harm in telling. He would write ten letters to everyone that he received from her. He was fearfully humble about her.

"You wouldn't expect a girl," he used to say "to write very often to such an ugly pup as I am." When he spoke like that he would grin self-derisively and purposely show all his gold stoppings. He went home on leave to England six months ago determined to make sure of her and to bring matters to a crisis. She met him with the news that she was going to be married to an officer whom we all knew to be a quitter. She begged him to be present at the wedding so that people might not talk. He went to the wedding and returned to the front six days ahead of time. Since then he's seemed to be more white and small and bowlegged than ever.

I'm the only man who knows what lies behind his life. We're the best of friends and, when we're in the line, we always sleep in the same dugout—which occasions a certain amount of jealousy among the other officers. When we're on the march, he has to follow the routine etiquette and share his billets with the captain. I hate to see him go up front for fear he should die. He shares the same fear for me, and is continually inventing excuses for getting me on the wire when I'm forward. God created him a caricature—the potter's thumb slipped in the moulding of his clay; but to make amends God gave him the heart of a lion. You love him, protect him, declare him "quaint," but never for a moment do you cease to admire him with a strangely simple and passionate loyalty. He's as straight as John the Baptist; it would be impossible to tell him a lie.

We have a race-horse in our battery which the major uses as his charger—a dainty, fine-boned aristocrat of a fellow, red and lean as a rusty sword. When our little major rides him, leading his battery down the long white roads of France, strangers halt to gaze at the almost childish figure with the short bowed legs, wondering how he ever contrived to climb up so high.

At the head of his battery, where he ought to appear most imposing, he looks more like a jockey than a field-officer. It doesn't matter what strangers wonder or what he looks like, now that we're bound on a death and glory adventure there's no man to whom we would sooner entrust or for whom we would sooner lay down our lives. We forget the carelessness of the potter's thumb and remember only the stoutness of heart which the feeble body hides. His name is Wraith—Charlie Wraith; and his age——. I should guess him to be thirty, though three and a half years of war have so battered his body that he looks forty-five.

At last the game ends. It's eleven o'clock; we march at midnight and can just reach the wagon-lines by short-cuts and hard riding. The major has been in luck; he's pocketing all the winnings. The glasses are filled for a final toast. The new major who is taking over from us, raises his glass, "Here's to Hell with the Kaiser and, if you've got to die, may you all die smiling."

We laugh as we make a no heeler of it; dying might be the merriest of sports. But to me—I can't help thinking of that laddie, a single day at the front, lying beneath a saddle-blanket with his throat cut and that amazed expression of protest in his staring eyes.

We've climbed out of the trench and stand looking down at the faces clustered in the angle formed by the lifted curtain. A few paces to my left a cross shows plainly, upon which is written, "Here lies an Unknown British Soldier." Unknown! A hundred years from now we shall all be unknown. We shall be massed together in an anonymous glory as "the heroes who stormed the Vimy Ridge." It won't mean any more to be remembered as John Smith than merely as "An Unknown British Soldier" who did his duty faithfully.

"Good-luck," the faces in the candle-light cry.

"Cheerio," we answer. But the words which are in all our minds are, "Those about to die, salute thee."

Waving our hands, we turn away. The old racehorse, Fury,

from a hundred yards has recognised his master's voice and whinnies. With a pat on the neck and some coaxing words we get mounted, and walk carefully through the pitfalls of craters till we strike the road, when we grip with our knees and set off at the gallop.

Beneath the moonlight the chalk of the shell-ploughed battlefield creates the illusion of a country under snow, spreading beneath the velvet darkness for miles. The horses are impatient and refuse to be reined in. They need no guiding. With Fury in the lead, they leap trenches and take short-cuts where we would hesitate.

Ahead of us through the shadows we discover the battery drawn up in line, not a light or so much as a cigarette showing for fear our doings should be betrayed to the enemy planes. Heming rides out as we approach. He salutes the major smartly. "Just in the nick of time, sir; our battery leads and we march as a brigade. There are no route orders. Everything's secret. The Colonel alone knows where we're going; even he doesn't know beyond tonight."

The adjutant gallops up and reins in importantly. "The Colonel's compliments, and he's waiting for you, sir. He wants to know what's the delay."

"No delay," says the major curtly, and wheels about to face the battery.

"Stand to your horses," he orders. "Gunners and drivers prepare to mount. Mount." There's a jingling of stirrups and the sound of men leaping to their places. As they sit to attention on the limbers and in the saddles, all grows silent.

"Column of route from the right. Walk. March," the major commands.

The horses of A Sub-section gun-team throw their weight into the collars. There's a commotion of prancing in the darkness and the merciless sound of the cracking of whips; then through the shadows the big bays of A Sub strain forward and take shape; the B. C. party gallops to the head of the column and we're off on our mysterious march in pursuit of the greatest of high adventures.

CHAPTER 8

The March Begins

There's no end of a thrill in night-marching, if one doesn't get too much of it. One feels curiously winged when mounted in the darkness, as though the limitations to speed, space and possibility had broken down. The present merges with the past and with eternity. Doors open in the night, giving entrance to previous incarnations. The mounted men are a robber-band; the guns are wagons piled with loot. The villages, lying flattened by shell-fire, are walled towns which hide medieval palaces. The country through which we pass, takes on a hundred exquisite and grotesque shapes, the one melting into the other at the bidding of the imagination.

Everything is unusual, everything is shifting, everything is distorted and capable of being changed at will. One has an extraordinary sense of timelessness and an overwhelming certainty that he has done all this before, marching to the sack of cities, and suffering weariness and death for unremembered causes. The ghosts of those forgotten tragedies and triumphs throng about him, bewildering him with a faint familiarity which he fails to associate with any land or clime.

On that first night-march we had to keep our column closed up to prevent straggling, since on asecret march to an unknown destination a straggler inevitably gets lost. If a vehicle had to halt to refit harness, to have a horse shod or for any other cause, we had to leave out-riders at every cross-road to guide it back to the main body.

The first part of our journey was through country we had fought over, every contour of which, despite the darkness, was pictured vividly in our minds. We passed the narrow valley behind the Maison Blanche, in which our battery had lain hidden up to the time when the Ridge was captured.

We passed the crossroads at the Ariane Dump, where we used to assemble midnight after midnight to build the artillery road up to the front-line, that our guns might pass forward across No Man's Land within four hours of the start of the offensive. Many spots were memorable to us because of men who had died. It was over there to the right that the Hun sniper got our signalling sergeant, when we were observing from behind the Five Hundred Crater. It was over there to the left that a Hun shell scored a direct hit on B. Sub's gun-pit and sent all the gun-detachment west. Though we were to forget these homes that we have had in the mud, our horses remember and remind us; each time they pass one of their old wagon-lines, they try to turn in off the road from force of habit.

Through the mist and moonlight we can just make out the twin towers, blunted and splintered, of Mount St. Eloi. They look like the thumb and index-finger of a solemn hand, pointing heavenward.

One tower is tall and defiant; the other has been shorn by shell-fire. The Huns commenced their work of destruction during the Franco-Prussian war; since this war started, they have done their utmost to complete it, even sending over bombing-planes for that purpose. They have a good military reason, for the towers command a panoramic view of forty miles of country. But still the towers stand, exclaiming in a valiant gesture of architectural oratory that God still dwells beyond the clouds.

In the hollow, between Mount St. Eloi and the road which we travel, lies God's Acre, with its endless forest of white crosses. It is there that very many of the pals who have served with us are taking their last rest. They are wrapped in the army blankets which made so many journeys with them. Each has a little scooped out hole, three feet beneath the ground and only just big enough to take his body. The blanket is pulled up over the face and hurriedly sewn into place for fear the sleeper should stir and be cold beneath the sod.

As I gaze through the darkness towards the hollow, I can feel the wounds of the sleeping men. There's Bennet with a bullet through the centre of his forehead; that happened when we were observing from Sap 29 in front of Ecurie. There's Gordon, who came back from a gay leave in Paris to have his leg shattered at the entrance to the Bentata Tunnel. How he made us laugh the night before he died with his account of "ze lady wiz ze vite furs," who tried to make him pay for her dinner at the Cafe de la Paix!

And there's Athol, who was brigade medical officer when we occupied the railroad in front of Farbus. Brigade headquarters were on the ridge and the batteries were in the plain. The moment he saw that we were being strafed, he would come racing down through the shell-fire to our assistance. He got smashed to atoms when he was binding up some of our chaps in a blown-in dugout; there was nothing but his face left undamaged. I wonder why it is that I still walk the earth while they sleep there so quietly.

We all took the same risks. We all dreamt of the same adventure—the adventure on which we now are bound—of the day when trench-warfare would end and we should break the German line, and take our guns into action at the gallop. Do they strain their ears where they lie so narrowly as they catch the rumble of our departing guns? Do they push back the earth from their sunken eyes, raising themselves on their elbows to listen? Dick Dirk is there by now—he who returned ahead of time from Blighty because he wanted to "go straight for her."

His house underground is newer than the others. Does he wish us luck, or does he pay us no attention? No, they do not stir. They lie heedless and silent. Having done their bit, they are contented, for they were very tired. As the hollow is swallowed up in the all-surrounding pool of night, I look back just once to where my dead companions rest, and again the words take shape in my mind, "Those about to die, salute thee."

We wheel out on to the straight pave road which runs like an arrow's flight from Arras to St. Pol. In a long and regular line on either side stand pollarded trees, marking its direction for miles. They seem gigantic sentinels, silent and impassive. From all directions, from main roads and bye-roads, comes the muffled roar of transport pouring along every artery of travel to the same unknown bourne to which we journey.

A tremendous movement of troops is taking place—taking place under cover of darkness, anonymously, timed absolutely and without hurry. If we doubted that a big offensive was on foot, we do not doubt it now. But whose is the controlling brain? Rumour says that even our corps commander has had no warning as to our ultimate destination. The sergeant-major rides back to tell me that the major wants me at the head of the column. I trot forward and find that he is walking, while his groom leads Fury a few paces behind. I salute, dismount and hand over my horse to a signaller.

Chapter 9

Hide & Seek

The major wants to talk—he feels lonely. We begin by making guesses as to the scope of the new offensive. We converse very quietly for fear we should be overheard by any of our men. A corps order has been published forbidding any discussion of the object of our present movements. Such discussion, if it takes place in public, comes under the heading of "Giving information to the enemy." It's impossible to say who of the people with whom we associate are spies. Many a good life has been thrown away as the result of careless and boastful conversations in estaminets and officers' tea-rooms.

Some bounder, out of the line for a day, wants to air his superior knowledge of doings up front; he talks with a raised voice in order to impress strangers who may or may not be in British uniforms. In any case, the uniform is no proof of integrity; many an English-speaking Hun has passed secretly through our lines in the uniform of the man he has murdered. The result of such loose speaking is that the raid, which ought to have succeeded, fails. The Huns are forewarned; their trenches are stiff with machine-guns and many of our men go west.

Every precaution is being taken this time that no information of importance to the enemy shall leak out. In the first place, we know nothing ourselves; in the second, we are forbidden to conjecture out loud. Though we recognise landmarks in the landscape, we are under orders not to mention the fact. We are only to march when night has blindfolded our eyes; our tongues, under pain of court-martial, are to be kept silent.

To judge by the north-easterly direction in which we are marching, we might be going up to Flanders to recapture the Hun gains at Kernel. The major believes, however, that our present direction gives no indication, as we're probably only going to a railroad junction at which we shall entrain. He thinks that our goal lies to the south. It may be the Rheims salient, in which case we shall be in entirely new territory, fighting with the French and joining up with the Americans, concerning whom we are exceedingly optimistic and curious. On the other hand there are rumours that the Americans are taking over from the French in the Argonne sector, thus releasing many French veteran troops who will be behind us to back us up in the counter-stroke of which we are the hammer-head. One fact is known definitely—Canadians have been sent north to Ypres; but whether to fool the Hun or because the thrust is to be made there, remains uncertain.

The Hun knows that the Canadians have been trained to be the point of the fighting-wedge; he, therefore, knows that where we are there the blow is to be struck. All summer he has made every effort to keep track of our position in the line, his object being that he may have his reserves rightly placed to push back our thrust. For the war on the Western Front has become entirely a game of the handling of reserves. Neither side has sufficient manpower to defend its trench-system if an attack were to take place all along its front.

So it remains for the attacker to muster his storm-troops with such stealth that the people to be attacked may be kept unaware of what is planned against them and may be tricked into withdrawing their reserves to a place remotest from the point where the blow is to fall. If such strategy succeeds, the attacker has the element of surprise in his favour and gains so much ground in the impetus of his first rush that, by the time the enemy reserves can be brought up, the entire defence has become disorganised.

The great aim of the new strategy is to make a gap—to get through the enemy so that his right and left flanks are out of touch and railroad communications in his rear can be cut.

The new strategy was first practised by our Third Army in its November drive against Cambrai; that drive failed for want of sufficient reinforcements to back it up. Until that time the Allies had always gone after what were known as "limited objectives," such as high ground, trench-systems, villages, salients. When the objective had been taken, the attack rested. The Vimy Ridge was a limited objective. We didn't want to break the Hun line; what we desired was the Ridge, because it commanded a great enemy plain on the other side.

For two months before we actually struck, we advertised the fact that we were going to strike by the intensity of our incessant shell-fire. Systematically, day by day and night by night, we cut the enemy's wire-entanglements, blew up his dumps, mined beneath his front-line, pounded his cement machine-gun emplacements, harassed his means of communication and stole his morale by making his life perilous and wretched. He knew as well as we did what was planned; his only uncertainty was as to the exact hour at which the attack was to be launched.

We kept him wearily guessing, and wore his nerves to a frazzle by putting on intense bombardments at inconvenient times. Usually these bombardments took place at dawn, lasted for fifteen minutes and had all the appearance of being the genuine zero hour. When our barrage had descended, he would man his trenches, call up his reserves and set all the machinery for his counter-thrust working. Then, as suddenly as it had started, the hell would die down into the intensest quiet.

The new strategy does not advertise the point to be attacked. It does not cut wire-entanglements with shell-fire many days before the show commences; it tramples down obstacles with battalions of tanks at the very moment that the infantry are advancing. It does not set out to capture a given and solitary object; its ambition is to double up the enemy's line and to penetrate as far as success will allow. The new strategy is in all things more stealthy, more tiger-like, more reckless, more deadly; its most dangerous feature is the use which it makes of surprise.

This new method of fighting has developed out of the necessity for defeating a heavily entrenched enemy. It is a method which the Allies at last are able to adopt because of the almost limitless resources in man-power which America has placed at their disposal. For the Western Front to be rightly understood, must be regarded as a banjo-string, composed of living men holding hands from Switzerland to the English Channel.

Under pressure the string may give and give, but it must never break. The moment it breaks, the thing happens which takes place when a banjo-string snaps—it curls up towards the ends and leaves a gap. The only power that can save the day when the banjo-string has snapped, is the masterly strategic employment of the reserves. The reserves may stop the rush by selling their lives to a man, or they may do it by luring the attacker on until he has advanced beyond his strength. But if the side attacked has guessed wrongly as to the point to be attacked, so that its reserves are at a distance when the disaster happens, a calamitous retreat on either flank will have to be begun or the jig is up. To compel this retreat is the purpose of Foch's present thrust.

In adopting these hide-and-seek tactics of night-marches we are borrowing a lesson from the Hun. He has already tried to do precisely what we now intend to accomplish. In his great drive of the spring, when he all but took Rheims and Amiens, he massed his storm-troops seventy miles behind his objective. Day by day he kept them hidden from spy and aeroplane observation, moving them only by night. His railroad and transportation arrangements were so perfect that, commencing at dusk, he was able to fling the whole weight of his fighting-wedge up front and have it hammering at our doors by daylight.

As we rode beneath the August night, my major summed up the situation: "We're trying to bluff the Hun into expecting us up north, while we make for the south as fast as we can hurry. I'll tell you what it is, Chris; we can afford to die, now that the Americans are behind us with their millions. Believe me, before this month is ended, there's going to be some tall dying."

That phrase, "We can afford to die," arrested my attention.

It was so brutally financial, as though human lives were only so much national capital, and not the focus-points of loyalties and affections. It was as though the casualties for the military year could be apportioned ahead of time, so that the national books of birth and death might be made to balance. It was making a mathematical calculation as to men's uncalculated and individual sacrifice; no more must be killed in any given twelve months than the bodies of the living could resupply.

And yet yes, it was true: for the first time in the history of the war we could afford to die. During the previous four years we had died, but we could not afford it. We had had to be careful about our deaths, so that our manpower might not sink below that of the enemy who faced us. Now at last, because the Americans were behind us, we could afford to become lavish in the spending of our lives. Where one British soldier fell, three American boys would spring up. Though we became sightless, soundless, nameless, trodden by shells into the oozing horror of the mud, other idealists of another nation, but still of our tongue and blood, would cross by the bridge our bodies had made, fighting on and up till the decency for which we had perished was won. Viewed in this light, the knowledge that we could afford to die became not brutal, but glorious.

The major whistled softly, strutting through the darkness on his little bowed legs. The thought that they could afford to let him die caused his spirits to rise.

CHAPTER 10

Bully Beef and Suzette

"Keep to the Right," and, after an interval, "Ha-alt!" Passed back down the unseen column ahead of us come the hoarse cries, followed by a sudden cessation of wheels and then, sharp and emphatic, "Dismount the drivers."

Our major shouts back the orders to the sergeant-major; from him they are picked up by the section-commanders and numbers one. We listen to them as they travel down the battery through the darkness, altered in tone and made more faint as each new voice takes up the cry. The B. C. party back their ridden and led animals into the grass on the side of the road, loosen the reins and allow their beasts to graze. This is the first halt that we have made, so it should be long enough to give us time to check over the fitting of the harness and to make sure that everything is correct. I climb into the saddle to ride down the line; as I turn away, the major calls to me, "Oh, Chris, one minute!" I bend down to catch his words: "Find out what's happened to Bully Beef and Suzette."

What's happened to Bully Beef and Suzette? That question has been in my mind, in the mind of the major, and probably in every gunner's and driver's mind ever since we marched out from the wagon-lines. It's dead against all army orders that a woman and child should accompany a fighting unit into action. Since the war started, camp-followers of whatever sort have been forbidden. From time to time, even the dogs in the army areas have been shot because many of them were spies, carrying messages to the Germans across No Man's Land at night. It's dead against every dictate of decency and humanity that fighting-men should take non-combatants with them into the kind of furious carnage towards which we ——. But, somehow, Bully Beef and Suzette do not seem to be non-combatants; we regard them as soldiers. They march with us as representatives of the impassioned soul of France. Yes, and more than that—for they stand to us for everything tender and kindly that would have been ours, had we not been selected to die. Suzette is to us what Joan of Arc must have been to her soldiers—the dream of the woman we would have married had Fate been more lavish with life. And Bully Beef—he's the might-have-been child of every boy and man in the battery.

Gun-carriages and wagons have been pulled well over to the right, clear of the pave road, so as not to cause a block in the passing traffic. It's difficult to see them in detail on account of the blackness caused by the wall of trees on either side. One can just make out the heads of horses and the huddled figures of men on the limbers, too tired to know that we have halted. Usually when I enquire, I find that the sleepers were on guard or picket the night previous. We let them sleep on. They are wise; none of us know how far we have to go or how many nights of wakefulness lie before us.

Behind the darkness I can hear the drivers lifting up the feet of their horses and feeling for stones. Good boys, these drivers! They love their beasts and speak to them as pals. There's so much discipline that one doesn't get much time for loving in the army. I remember a march on this same road when the drivers were so frozen that they had to be lifted out of their saddles; no one had the strength to unfasten a bit till he had thawed his fingers be-tween the horse's back and the saddle-blanket. Yet there wasn't one man who quit when we limped into our muddy standings. Every gunner and driver went to work on the horses, grooming them with a will and trying to make them comfortable before he thought of himself—and this, not because it was ordered, but because he realised through his own misery the forlornness of his four-footed comrades.

Good boys, all of them! I think the Lord of Compassion, when the final reckoning comes, will remember kindnesses even to horses. When he judges those drivers, he'll not forget the bitter cold of that winter's march and what it meant to stand grooming in the snow and sleet when you were bitten to the bone and almost crying with misery. So he'll pass over their swearing and the times when they got drunk, and he'll say, pointing to the horses who will also be in Heaven, "*Inasmuch as ye did it unto the least of these, my brethren, ye did it unto me.*" If that should happen, the drivers will be most awfully surprised, because according to their standards they only did their duty.

Some of the chaps in my section, which is the leading and senior section of the battery, try to ask me questions as I pass.

"Are we going far, sir?"

"Are we going out for training?"

"Do you think, sir, that it's the Big Push at last?"

I cannot see their faces, but I recognise them by their voices. They are drawn from every class of society. Some of them were college boys, some were mechanics, some day-labourers, some adventurers, some came out of gaol to join. Now only one quality lifts one man above another his courage. Their questions are asked from all kinds of motives friendliness, curiosity, nervousness. I am conscious of an atmosphere of tension throughout the battery. It seems a shame that they should be told nothing. In no other game in the world would you march men to their death, without so much as warning them that it was to their death that they were going. From one of my questioners a man who was wounded eight months ago and has just rejoined us I pick up a significant piece of information.

"I can see you're not telling, sir, but I know. It's to the Big Push that we're going. And here's why I know when we left England, they were emptying every camp sending drafts to France secretly every night. When I got to our Corps Reinforcement Camp, not thirty kilometres from here, I found the place so jammed that you could hardly find a space to spread your blanket. With the men they have there, the corps must be fifty *per cent* over-strength. That means just one thing, sir that we're getting ready for fifty *per cent* casualties."

"Perhaps," I answer him, "but, if I were you, I wouldn't talk about it."

I reach the centre section, which Tubby Grain is commanding. Tubby is a plump little officer and rides a wicked little Indian pony as well-fleshed as himself.

"The major's compliments, and he wants you to look over your section and report on it," I tell him.

His reply is, as usual, insubordinate and cheery. "Holy, jumping cat-fish! What does the major think I am? Don't I always look over my section when there's a halt?" And then confidentially, " I say, old top, what about Bully Beef and Suzette?"

I tell him that I'm on my way to find out. As I ride away he shouts after me the latest catchword from Blighty, "How's your father?"

To which, if you are in the know, the proper reply is, "Very well, thanks. He still has his baggy pants on." I'm in too much of a hurry to give the correct countersign, so Tubby facetiously sends a mounted bombardier after me, who catches me up while I'm speaking to Gus Edwine, the commander of the left and rear section. The bombardier salutes without a smile and sits to attention, waiting for me to take notice of him in the darkness.

"Well, what is it, bombardier?"

"Mr. Grain's compliments, sir, and if you meet his father, would you tell him that he really ought to have his baggy pants on these cold nights."

Gus gaffaws and steals my dynamite by sending a return message: "My compliments to Mr. Grain, and tell him that it's all right; Suzette is repairing his father's baggy pants."

Then to me, "But how about Suzette? I went to look for her three hours before we left the wagon-lines; her bivouac was pulled down, and she and Bully Beef weren't anywhere in sight. I didn't like to ask because . . . Well, you know, if we're going to buck army regulations, there are some things that most of us shouldn't know too much about. If the general or the colonel asks questions and you don't know, you can't tell. Ignorance saves a lot of lying."

At the tail of the column I find the transport the G. S. wagons, the water-cart, the officers' mess-cart, the cook-cart, the shoeing-smith's cart looking humpy and nomadic as a travelling circus. The prisoners are there on foot with their escort, A group of stragglers are regaining their wind before reporting back to their proper sections. Mongrel curs, which we have adopted in our travels, yap down at me from the tarpaulin-covered mountains of stores or run sniffing about the heels of the horses. This house-keeping portion of our military life is in the care of the captain. It is here, if anywhere, that I shall get the news I want.

I find Heming with the quartermaster, directing the repacking of some bales of hay which have shifted with the bumping of the journey. It always makes me smile to watch him engaged upon an unimaginative and practical task; he still has the aloofness of the artist. Beneath his khaki I can still discover the privileged dreamer whom the world flattered and who scarcely knew how to tie his own shoe-lace. He has compelled himself to become practical; but if the war were to end tomorrow, he would at once cease to be a soldier and fall back into his old way of life. I believe in his secret heart it is just that falling back that he dreads; out here he has learnt to be lean as a rapier. He loathes the thought of again becoming self-applauding and flabby. If the price of keeping lean is "going west" on the battlefield, he is perfectly content. To quote his own words, "There's nothing leaner than a skeleton."

"Captain Heming!"

"Hulloa, Chris! Pretty black, isn't it? I didn't see you. What's your trouble?"

"A message from the major." I sink my voice. "He wants to know what you've done about Bully Beef and Suzette?"

"Suzette!" I can't see his face. As he pronounces her name, he sucks the air through his teeth the way a man does when he shudders. Then, "Look here, does the major really want to know what I've done with them?"

"He told me to find out."

"But if he knows, he ought to take action. If he doesn't take action, he becomes my accomplice and may get into trouble with those higher up. He'd better take it for granted that we left them behind at Vimy, unless. . ."

"Unless what?"

"Unless he really does wish that we had left them behind."

"So so we didn't leave them behind?"

"Hand your horse over to one of the chaps," he says; "you shall see for yourself."

We go on foot towards the wagon on which the bales of hay were being repacked. The job is all finished now; the tarpaulin has been pulled tightly over the top and roped down. The quartermaster is standing in rear of the wagon as though he were on guard. He's an old soldier who has fought through many wars; he wears the African ribbon and several Indian decorations. He's a big, comfortable sort of man, with an immense stomach and a body over six foot high. He has a wart on the right side of his nose, which he rubs thoughtfully when he talks to you. His voice is thick, as though his throat were grown up with fat.

Of all our non-commissioned officers he's the kindest. He plays the part of a father to the chaps, and has saved many a young soldier from going on the wrong slant. His name is Dan Turpin "Big Dan." The only beast of sufficient strength to carry him is an ex-Toronto fire-engine horse, called "Little Dan" not that he is little, but to distinguish him from his master. As we approach, Big Dan is singing to himself in a sepulchral voice,

Old soldiers never die
They simply fade away.

It would take more than a drive against the Huns to get Dan's wind up.

"Quarter!"

"Yes sir."

We hear his heels click together and the jingle of his spurs.

"Is the wagon repacked all right?"

"All correct, sir."

"Just loosen the flap of the tarpaulin at the back; I want to see for myself."

The rope securing the flap is untied and we slip our heads under the tarpaulin. Carefully, so that none of the light may spill on to the road and give us away to aeroplanes, Heming turns on his flash. At first the illumination is blinding; then one sees that the bales of hay have been so stacked as to leave a hollow. Inside the hollow someone stirs, sighs and turns over, disturbed by the light. The figure is slight and covered by an officer's trench-coat. Heming shifts the flash, so that it creeps along the body and reveals the face. Suzette! Her khaki tunic is unhooked and un-buttoned at the neck. Bully Beef lies snuggled in her arms, with his small head hidden against her breast. Her soldier's cap has slipped aside and her hair, which was like honey and sunshine, has been cut square against the neck. From beneath the trench-coat I see that she is wearing *puttees*. I understand she will pass for a man now.

But why does she want to accompany us into danger? Is she so desperately alone and fed-up with life? And Heming, why does he ? She opens her eyes and smiles sleepily, knowing that we are friends.

From farther up the column we hear the order being shouted back, "Get mounted the drivers."

The flash goes out. "Goodnight, Suzette." The tarpaulin is lowered and tied into place. From far ahead comes the groaning of guns and ammunition-wagons taking up the march.

All night as I ride, there burns in my brain the picture of that refugee French girl with her fatherless child, journeying with us towards the calvary from which all the civilian world is fleeing. She is escaping towards death. And I think of another mother, no less a soldier-woman, who fled by Eastern highways that she might bring her son back to the death from which she fled, in order that men might live better.

Suzette! Why does she accompany us? She knows that we

need her love, perhaps. That knowledge brings her very near to the peasant mother of Nazareth.

CHAPTER 11

At Point of Exhaustion

The dawn stole upon us like a ghost. It ran beside us, fell behind, dashed on ahead, following and peering from behind trees and ruins. Along the endless road we crawled, weary and spent. The gunners had been ordered to dismount from the limbers to ease the horses' load. The out-riders and officers for the sake of example, had also dismounted and walked ahead of their chargers. All talking had ceased. We stumbled forward like somnambulists, pale and heavy-eyed. Had anyone been told that we were storm-troops, Foch's Pets, the hammer-head of the attack, moving up to smash the Hun line, he would have laughed. We looked listless, washed out. Now and then a man would ask an officer, "How much further, sir?"

The officer would reply, "I don't know. Not much further, I should think." The man's head would sag forward again on his breast. In the army there is no complaining, no going on strike; one carries on and on till he drops. To carry on, however harsh the demands, and not to drop is one's pride.

As day grew whiter and the sunrise reddened, we learnt a good deal about the condition of affairs that night had masked. Every few yards through the standing wheat new lines of defences had been dug. Trench-system behind trench-system stretched for miles, scarring the greenness of the landscape. They were all of recent construction, for the earth had been but newly turned. Here, behind a wood or a rise of ground, a battery position had been selected and gun-pits laid out. One came to what looked like a hay-stack or a pile of tumbled logs, only to find that it was a machine-gun nest, cunningly chosen to command a valley down which an advancing enemy must march. Beneath grass in ditches wire-entanglements had been hidden, so contrived that they could be set up across the road at a moment's notice, to obstruct pursuing cavalry. One could follow the reasoning of the stealthy mind which had woven this maze of destruction.

The enemy would have maps of our back-country worked out from their aeroplane photographs. They would know beforehand each dip and hollow where artillery and machine-gun resistance might be expected; consequently they would try to neutralise such resistance with their heavies before they sent their infantry forward. The stealthy mind had argued every probability; very often it had arranged its strong points in open places, where the position was so badly chosen that it would not be suspected.

It became plain that whatever our game might be, this time it was to be neck or nothing. The Allies might be planning to attack; but, if they had to retire, they were reckoning on selling every yard of land at the highest cost in lives. All the machinery for the shambles was ready, only the bodies were lacking. One did not require to be highly imaginative to picture the murder holes these woods and valleys would become when once the slaughter started. For someone disaster was brewing; whether for ourselves or the Germans, it was impossible to guess.

Now that it was daylight, we recognised the country; it had been quiet and unwarlike when last we had passed through it. The rapid transformation enabled us to realise the terror of the fighting which had been taking place to the south the desperate few, digging their toes in, determined not to budge, British, American, French, hanging on in the hope of reinforcements which could not come. The landscape lying smiling in the August dawn lost its peacefulness; one saw it as it might become a hell ensanguined by death, through which men crawled from rifle-pit to rifle-pit like dogs with their spines broken.

Wherever the eye rested, fear threatened and muttered. The

doubt sprang up that even we might be defeated. They marched us to and fro under sealed orders. They made us die and suffer; but they told us nothing. Who were they these people who never spoke to us or saw us, these people whose lives were too valuable to endanger? They lived miles behind the lines in chateaux. They slept in sheeted beds. They ate as much as they liked. They took two leaves to Blighty to our one. Their breasts were covered with decorations. They never knew the weariness of night-marches; staff-cars whisked them between breakfast and lunch across distances that it took us a week to trudge.

What right had they to all this consideration? Were they really so wise as they thought they were? If they bungled, it was we who had to pay; it was our bodies that would be mangled; our blood, needlessly expended, that would wash out their errors. And when in spite of bad staff-work our courage had conquered, it would be we who would get whatever blame was coming and they who would get the credit.

In the centre section a horse fell down; it had gone to sleep while in draught. The driver must have been at fault; he, too, was probably nodding. From down the column Tubby Grain's voice reached us, angrily strafing in unprintable language. The commotion grew fainter as the other teams swung out into the road and the column passed on.

At a bend we came across a Chinese labour battalion, shuffling up to work on the trenches. Across their shoulders they balanced poles, with the load tied on either end. Their clothing was nondescript the refuse of every rag-shop of Europe and the Orient. The proudest Chinaman of the lot swaggered and sweltered in the remains of a great-coat, which had belonged to an officer in the Prussian Guard. They went by us clacking their tongues and laughing, happy as children if one of our chaps smiled back. Beside them, rigid and regimental, marched their British non-commissioned officers, hard, uncheerful men of the Indian service, who carried rods with which to enforce obedience.

A cruel war! A war to the point of exhaustion when the white man, that his God might be defended, had to rouse Confucius from his long contemplation. These men, they tell us, have been recruited from districts in China which have been stricken with famine. They have exchanged their rice-fields and pagodas for the bombed areas and dugouts of war not for our sakes, but that their yellow wives and children may not starve.

You can find representatives from all the world marching up to the trenches along the dusty roads of France. We Canadians have Japanese in our British Columbia battalions; our sharp-shooters are Red Indians. The New Zealanders have Maoris; the South Africans Kaffirs; the West Indians Negroes; the cavalry Sikhs. All mankind is here for one reason or another for gain, adventure, principle, patriotism; but chiefly that they may prove that it was not in vain that Christ grew up in Nazareth. There are aborigines from the Pacific Islands, one generation removed from cannibals; Arab horsemen who have worshipped Allah in the desert; savages from the jungle; wanderers by divers trails, who had lost their way in the maze that leads out to civilization. They have all been sent here by their indignant gods that they may drag down the more brutal god of the Germans.

We drowse; we crawl; we halt. Again we move forward. Our eyes are aching with sleeplessness. We pass by a prison-camp, surrounded by a huge cage, inside of which Hun prisoners are lined up to get their breakfast. Our mouths are dry and we view their steaming mess-tins with envy.

We march on, scarcely interested now in our direction. Heels are blistered. Where we are going no longer matters, if they would only give us time to rest. Of a sudden there's a cheering at the head of the column. Men pull themselves together. There's been no order passed down that we should march to attention, but every gunner is marching close behind his vehicle and the drivers are sitting upright in their saddles.

Far up the road, on the banks on either side, are standing men who wear a strange uniform. Their slouch hats at a distance look a little like the Australians', but their tunics are much tighter. Before ever we come abreast of them, the word has been whispered back, "They're here—the Americans!" There's no sleepiness about us now. The blistered feet are forgotten; we're marching like soldiers.

"They're here—the Americans!" It's fifteen months since we heard that they were coming. We've sung their promise,

Over there, over there,
Send the word, send the word over there,
That the Yanks are coming—

We've waited and we've hoped and many of the boys who hoped have died. We've heard that they were present at the great retreat before Cambrai in 1917. We've been told that they were coming by their thousands, but as yet we have seen none of them. Hun prisoners have consistently assured us that there were no Americans in France—that they were not coming. Now we are to see the Yanks with our own eyes.

"Battery, eyes front. March to attention—" the order passes smartly down the column.

We go by them, looking neither to left nor to right—so, after all, we can scarcely be said to have seen them. They are coloured troops tremendous chaps with flashing teeth and rolling eyes. Our first Americans!

We no longer remember the wire-entanglements, the gun-emplacements and the new trench-systems which are being constructed by Chinamen so many miles back of the line. Our tails are up. We shan't retreat. The Yanks are no longer coming. They have come. We know now whither we are marching to the end of the war and to conquest.

The village into which we marched this morning is an old friend; we were billeted here earlier in the summer when we were withdrawn from the line for training. It consists of, perhaps, a hundred grey farmhouses clustered together in a willow-swamp. In the willow-groves nightingales were still singing when we entered.

In the swamp the River Scarpe has its source. At this point it is so weak and narrow that a boy could leap across it; the village geese touch bottom as they breast its ripples; a brigade of artillery could drink it dry if all the horses were led down together. Here it is peaceful, but to the south of Arras it becomes sufficiently broad to give its name to the valley through which the Hun tried to drive last spring, when the waters of the Scarpe ran scarlet.

The houses of the village stand at irregular intervals, divided from the road by a strip of common upon which geese graze. One reaches the common by little bridges which cross the Scarpe, which wanders singing, paralleling the highway. Nothing has been marred by shell-fire; the roar of the guns is so distant that it is seldom heard by day—only at night does their flash flicker momentarily, like the glow of a lantern carried between trees.

It is a very quiet spot, well within the threatened area, where war is ignored and life has not altered its ways. Nature has conspired with the inhabitants in pretending that the world is unchanged. The gardens are fragrant with flowers; there are even more birds than formerly, for the refugee songsters from No Man's Land have made these thickets their place of escape. The only terror that comes near to disturb them is the sullen explosion of bombs dropped at night from Hun planes, as is witnessed by raw scars in the greenness of the surrounding meadows.

When we entered, the white mists of morning still hung above the common; early risen cocks with their attendant harems were our only welcomers. We had set up our horse-lines and were half way through the grooming before the villagers discovered that old friends were again among them.

All day we have been wondering why we have been brought here. A part of the general plan of deception, I suppose—so that the Hun may think, if he hears of our whereabouts, that we've simply marched out for manoeuvres as before. All kinds of details confirm our belief that the big push is about to start. A divisional staff-car called in at brigade this noon; the Canadian maple leaf and all the usual divisional marks had been painted out. The patches and shoulder-badges of the car's occupants had been torn off—nothing was left that would betray the fact that storm-troops are on the march. As yet we have received no orders as to how long we are to stay here—it would be normal to give us a few days' rest; but none of the kit has been removed from the vehicles—which is significant. We could hook in and be off within the hour.

It was announced this morning that no more letters from our corps would be accepted at the army post office. This is the most certain sign we have had that an attack is going to be pulled off. Letters home are a frequent source of leakage of information. When men know that they are writing what may prove to be their last message to their mothers, wives, sweethearts, it is almost impossible for them to keep that knowledge to themselves. Moreover, we each one have codes, pre-arranged with our correspondents, by means of which we can get forbidden news past the censor—so it's wise, if harsh, to insist on silence between ourselves and the outside world.

The outside world! How little it understands what our lives are like. In the outside world there are standards of freedom and politeness; in all personal matters a man has the power of choice. He is at liberty to make or ruin himself. He washes if he so desires; if he prefers to go dirty, he does not wash. Within reason, as far as is compatible with the earning of his daily bread, he sleeps as long as he wants. To miss one's night's rest is to court ill-health. To be verminous is to fall into the category of the slum-dweller; to go hungry is well-nigh impossible. To lay down one's life for somebody else is exceptional and martyr-like. To become a criminal is a really difficult affair.

With us everything is reversed. We grow moustaches under army orders; we crop our hair to please the colonel. We have no areas of privacy either in our bodies or our souls. We rise, sleep, eat and wash when we are commanded. We are physically examined, physicked, pumped full of anti-toxins and marched off to church parade to worship God without our wishes being consulted. To die for someone else is not martyr-like, but our job. To go foodless, sleepless, shelterless and wet is not a matter for self-pity, but our accepted lot. We cannot give notice to our employers; we have no unions—no means of protest. To be always cheerful and smiling, the more cheerful and smiling in proportion to the hardship, is a duty for the performance of which we must expect no thanks.

Our existence as individuals is ignored until we have fallen short, then, all of a sudden, we become important. What in civilian life would be errors in taste or mistakes in temper with us are offences and crimes. For a man in the ranks to come upon parade unshaven, with his buttons unshone or a few minutes late is an office offence. To be found kicking a horse is a crime, demanding a court-martial. To strike a superior, to be asleep on sentry-go, or to be absent from the unit when it is moving into action means death.

Military punishments are largely physical and therefore degrading. They compel men to do better through fear of further punishment; they neither educate into a finer appreciation of righteousness, nor do they achieve any economic purpose. They consist in being strapped to a gun-wheel for so many hours a day or in being marched with heavy packs on the back when other men are resting. In the allotting of punishment the age, former social status or mental qualities of the offender are rarely taken into account. There are no excuses, no explanations.

Take the gravest crime of all—cowardice. In peace times it was generally allowed that not every man was brave. Before anyone who had been unheroic was judged, his history and environment were taken into consideration. But in the army if a man fails in courage he is shot. Had St. Peter been a soldier of the Allies, after denying Christ thrice he would never have been given the Keys of Heaven. He would have been executed at the feet of the hanging Judas. The army asks every man to be infallible; it can afford to show no mercy and gives no second chance. We are judged and graded by our military virtues. What we knew, were or possessed, and what has been our individual sacrifice of happiness count for nought. We are fighting-men, and therefore not required to think—only to obey blindly.

I suppose I still retain my civilian mind, for I cannot treat men as automatons; I have to interpret them with imagination. If one were to see only their externals, they would appear to be rough chaps, coarse in speech and habits, with a scowling attitude towards authority which only an iron discipline can keep subordinate. But when you view them with imagination, you see their enthusiasm for an ideal, which made them willing to give up their freedom and jeopardise their lives. For no one in our brigade needed to be in France; they all came as volunteers.

You also see how from the very first the army has failed to appreciate or make use of that enthusiasm; it prefers to treat men as people who, having signed away their bodies and lives, have to obey because they cannot escape. Yet despite the army, the enthusiasm of the men survives. It creeps out in their letters to their mothers and wives, to whom they still are heroes. It even creeps out in their conversation, when one's up front with them and keeping watch through the dreary hours of the night. They are coarse and rough it is true, for they are leading a coarse and a rough existence. Their only bedding is their blanket; they can never remove their clothes at night. Their chances for bathing come very rarely. They can carry only one change of under-clothing as their rolls have to be of an exact and limited size.

While in the line their quarters consist of holes burrowed under-ground; when out at rest they consist of broken down stables and barns, into which they are packed so closely that they can scarcely turn over without disturbing the men on either side. All the niceties and decencies of civilised life are denied them; war is a nasty affair and its nastiness cannot be avoided. No outcast of the city streets, drowsing under bridges and being harried by the police, leads a more comfortless existence. At the end of the journey, as a reward for their sufferings, are probable mutilation and death.

Is it to be wondered that some of them get drunk to escape their misery whenever the chance presents itself, and that when drunk, they become bold to challenge the discipline which in action is their greatest protection? The crimes which they commit are crimes only in the army—few of them would be even offences anywhere else. A man suffers the death penalty on active service for an error which in a civil court would cost him no more than a warning and a fine.

I can never get out of my mind the contrast between the individual magnanimity of each Tommy's sacrifice and the unimaginative callousness with which it is accepted. The self-denial of the men in the ranks is always far in excess of the self-denial of their officers. The higher an officer climbs in rank, the greater is his authority and the less his self-denial, yet the stronger grows his contempt for those beneath him. War conducted from a *chateau* and a Rolls Royce car is a comparatively pleasant affair; there is no temptation to get drunk or become a deserter. But war conducted from a front-line trench, upon bully beef, shell-hole water and hard tack, in a shirt that has been lousy for a month, with a body which is unwashed, unwarmed and famished for want of sleep—that kind of war is hell.

This is the kind of war that the man in the ranks fights with a grin upon his lips and a fierce determination to meet every calamity with a jest. The man in the ranks is the best man on the Front when he's at his best; there's no brass hat or red tab safe behind the lines who's worthy to touch the stretcher which carries him to his last, long rest. The red tab carries out laws for the private's punishment; he strafes him on review and goes out of his way to find faults; he makes him take to the ditch when his staff-car splashes by; he plans an offensive and sends him over the top to be smashed by shell-fire; if the offensive succeeds, he is awarded decorations for an ordeal through which he has not passed; the fighting Tommy wins the decorations, but the red tab wears them; and if at last the fighting Tommy's nerve forsakes him, it is the red tab who turns his thumbs down, confirming the sentence that he shall face the firing-squad.

Yet the private is the better man every hour of the day and in his heart the red tab knows it—knows it and resents it. If the war is won, it will be won by the sacrifice of simple men, who never wore a ribbon or any insignia of rank, but were content to die humbly and unnoticed. I love them, these gunners and drivers of mine—and I marvel at their patience. We are marching to a life and death conflict in which we take it for granted that every man in our command will live up to the most heroic standards, yet today at noon we held office.

The prisoners were marched in under escort, their heads bare and their arms held flatly to their sides. Most of the charges against them were paltry. This man had been caught with his candle burning after lights out had sounded; the next had been late upon early morning parade; the next had lost his box-respirator—he said it had been stolen; the next had been found riding on an ammunition-wagon after the order had been passed down the column for the gunners to dismount.

Not one of the offences alleged amounted to more than a misdemeanour, yet these men who are the picked storm-troops of the British Armies and whom we expect to face the shambles without flinching within the next few days, upholding the best traditions of the Empire, were marched hatless under an armed guard through the village street, with all the French girls staring at them. Some of them escaped punishment—some were awarded extra fatigues, pack-drill, additional pickets; many of them will be dead before their sentences have been served. We ask too much when we treat them as feudal slaves and expect them to act like crusaders.

Four years ago they were freemen—professional men, prairie-farmers, ranchers, lumber-jacks, surveyors. They wilfully forewent their liberty that an ideal might conquer. It is the fact that they were freemen in the truest sense that makes them fight so bravely. They were men accustomed to take risks, to stand upon two legs and confront Nature unafraid. We may treat them as schoolboys, but it is their triumphant manhood that gives them their dash and splendid self-reliance up front.

In other words, we try to crush the very spirit by our discipline which makes us victorious in battle. It seems strange that, knowing this to be the case, we should persist in governing them as people possessed of no intelligence.

Discipline is necessary—it is our stoutest safeguard in action; but it works unfairness in individual cases. Take for example the man unfortunately named Trottrot, who is one of the drivers in my section. Trottrot "got in bad" at the very start of the war; and he was in at the start—one of the first of the Canadian artillery-men to arrive in France. I think the trouble began with his name; some wag saw in it a chance for jocularity. Wherever he went men shouted after him "Where the hell did Trottrot trot?" I suppose his life was made so miserable that he lost his self-respect and did not care what happened.

At any rate his crime-sheet became famous throughout the Canadian corps. A man's crime-sheet is the record of his punishments from the first day he becomes a part of the army; it accompanies him from unit to unit and is his reference. His was as long and full of incident as a De Morgan novel. He had bucked authority in every way and suffered about every penalty short of being shot. To read it was a romance and an education. He had been absent without leave, drunk, insubordinate, late upon parade, had struck an officer, kicked more than one N. C. O. in the face and had spent six months of his service in a penal-settlement.

When he was attached to our battery a groan went up. No one wants to have a "bad actor" in a unit—his example is likely to become contagious. We tried to get out of taking him and, when that failed, had him brought before us. He was a slim, inoffensive looking youth, with pale eyes and a narrow, clever face. The major was seated at a table, fingering his voluminous crime-sheet, while we junior officers formed a half-circle behind him.

When Trottrot had been marched in by the sergeant-major and ordered to "Right-Turn," and was standing stiffly at attention, the major looked up.

"Driver Trottrot," he said, "you've got the name for being the worst man in the Canadian corps. If you go much further, you'll end by being shot. Of course that's entirely your own affair, but I'd like to help you to avoid it. I'm going to give you a new chance. I'm going to forget all about this Nick Carter novel you've been compiling." He tapped the man's crime-sheet and threw it aside. "I'm going to treat you as though you hadn't a stain on your record—as though you were a white man. As long as you play white by me, I'll treat you like a white man. The moment you act yellow, God help you. You're dismissed—that's all I have to say."

Driver Trottrot was handed over to me and I had a private talk with him. He would give no assurances that he was going to reform; he distrusted me the way a dog does a man who holds a whip behind his back. Little by little, however, as days went by he began to respond to kindness. Within a month he was the smartest man upon parade, had the cleanest set of harness and the best groomed horses. He was promoted to a centre-team, then to a wheel-team and was finally made lead-driver of the first-line wagon. Beyond this we have not dared to promote him because the men declare that he is not to be trusted under shell-fire. There are two ammunition-wagons to each gun: the firing-battery wagon, which follows the gun into action, and the first-line which brings up the ammunition.

The picked drivers of any sub-section are on the gun-teams, as their work is likely to prove the most dangerous; the next best are on the teams of the firing-battery; the next on those of the first line; the remainder are kept as spare drivers. The best driver of any team rides in lead. Trottrot ought to be driving lead of the gun by virtue of his work. Whenever an inspecting officer is going the round of our horse-lines, he always stops to praise the glossy coats of Trottrot's team and to comment on them as an example of what can be done by horsemanship. But we're afraid to give him his deserts on account of the men's belief that he lacks "guts." Trottrot has lived down his reputation for being a "bad actor," but his reputation for being "yellow" clings.

We treat him like a "white man." and he acts as though he were one. Perhaps the carnage towards which we are marching may give him his chance to wipe the slate clean of his old record. I hope so and believe that that's what he's hoping. There's a curious look of determination in his eyes, as though he waited breathless for the commencement of the danger. It's as though he were trying to tell me: "I won't let you down, sir, I'll either die in this show or come out of it lead-driver of the gun." I lay my money on Trottrot; he's a white man to his marrow, if I know one.

CHAPTER 12

Tragedy

After writing my prophecy concerning Driver Trottrot, I lay down to snatch a few hours sleep. My batman had spread my sleeping-sack on the tiled floor of the cottage bedroom in which I and three of my brother officers were billeted. The other three had been breathing heavily for some hours, wearied by the night's march. They had not removed more than their boots and tunics for fear we should receive hurried orders to take to the road again. They lay curled up like dogs, with their knees drawn to their chins, for all the world like aborigines who had scooped a hole in the leaves of a forest. One learns to sleep that way on active service and to lose no time in tumbling off. My last memory was of wide-open lattice-windows, the heavy listlessness of garden-flowers and the perfumed stillness of trees drowsing in the sultry August sun.

I was wakened by someone shaking my arm, and opened my eyes to find Driver Trottrot bending over me. His expression was a little alarmed at the liberty he was taking. "I wasn't told to come to you, sir," he explained quickly; "but I thought you ought to know. The boys were paid after morning stables, before they'd had anything to eat. A lot of these Frenchies started selling them *vin blink*. What with having had no sleep and then getting that stuff on their empty stomachs, they're getting fighting drunk. It's none of my business, but I thought you ought to stop it."

"Good for you, Trottrot," I said. "Chuck me over my boots;

I'll be with you in half a second."

For a moment I had a mind to rouse the other officers, but they looked so fagged that I determined to let them sleep on. I finished buttoning my tunic and buckling my Sam Browne as I hurried across the common. We passed over the little bridge, consisting of a single plank, and struck the road which led towards the horse-lines and the centre of the village.

As we walked I questioned Trottrot, trying to tap the experience he possessed as the ex-professional "bad man" of the Canadian corps. "Why do the chaps do things like this? Getting drunk isn't enjoyable and the after effects must be rotten."

"Chaps get drunk for various reasons," he answered. "They do it to forget; it isn't all honey being a gunner or a driver, and kicked around by everybody. They do it because some N. C. O. or officer has got a grouch against them, and picks on them so that they can't do anything right. They do it because they get tired of going straight; polishing harness and grooming horses three times a day is monotonous. They do it because there's nothing else to do, and they do it because they're lonely. Some does it because they likes it—it makes them feel that they own the world for a little while and are as good as anybody. And then there's those that does it because they're frightened."

"How do you mean, frightened?"

"Well, sir, the war's been going on for four years and it looks as though it might go on for twenty. A good many of us chaps have been wounded several times; we've not been killed yet, but we feel that our luck can't last. Each new attack that we come through lessens our chances. We know that sooner or later we're going to get it—and then it's pushing daisies for us, with nobody caring much. This new attack is worse than the others; we're told nothing and can only imagine. It isn't good to imagine. It's the suspense and the guessing that wears one. It's different for you, sir, than it is for us—you have to set an example. It's much harder just to follow. One has an awful lot of time for thinking on a long night march—he sees himself all messed up. It's to stop thinking that most chaps get drunk."

We were in the village by now, approaching the horse-lines. From the pretty cottages, which had looked so innocent in the early morning, came sounds of coarse laughter and discordant singing. Groups of men, swaying on their feet and arguing with uncouth, threatening gestures, tried to stand absurdly to attention and salute as we passed. "*Vin blink*," as the Tommies call the poisonous concoction which is sold them as "white wine," was doing its worst. No *poilu* would pour it down his gullet.

Whatever it is made of, it acts like acid and works like poison in the blood; especially is this the case with men who have been free from alcohol up front and are wearied in mind and body. A good deal of the traffic is carried on during prohibited hours and by unlicensed persons, at exorbitant rates and with a criminal disregard for consequences. Yet if property is damaged or a civilian assaulted the last centime of indemnity is exacted, the claims being pressed against defendants who are again in the line, making life safe for the relentless plaintiffs. Temptation is made easy for the Tommy; under the influence of "*vin blink*" he causes most of his trouble. A girl is usually the bait; she stands woodenly smiling in the doorway of her particular estaminet that he may see her as his unit enters a village. During all the four years of fighting this peculiarly cowardly form of profiteering has been going on. Nothing effectual has been done to stop it.

This being a village in which we had formerly been billeted, our men had required no one to give them pointers. At the morning stables they had been warned to keep sober and get all the sleep that was possible; but the moment they were dismissed, they had scattered to the various cottages where drink was obtainable. By this time many of them were mellow and some were completely intoxicated. On arriving at the horse-lines we found them lying beneath the guns and wagons and on the bales of hay, either dead to the world or staring dreamily at nothing. "One sees himself all messed up. It's to stop thinking that most chaps get drunk!"

Poor laddies! They were little more than boys. Life hadn't been over-gay for them since war started; by all accounts it would be even less gay in the coming months. Their faces told the story; boys of twenty looked forty. Their cheeks were hollow and lined; in their eyes was a strained expression of haggard expectancy. They were brave; they always would be brave. Their pride of race kept them up. Directly the battle had really started they would become alert and eager as runners.

But for the moment they had broken training; the long tension had proved too much. They had seized their opportunity for forgetfulness. Throughout the fields and beneath the trees, wherever there was a bit of shade they lay fallen and crumpled, their tunics flung aside and their shirts torn open to the chest. They would look very much like this one day when the tornado of bullets and shell-fire had swept over them. The thought made me sick; the picture was too horribly similar and realistic. It was only when I looked at the horses, strung out in three long lines, peacefully swishing their tails and nosing round for any wisps of hay that were remaining, that I felt assured that the catastrophe which was always coming nearer, had not yet befallen.

The important task before us was to get them collected up and safely into billets, where they could sleep off the effects of their debauch. Any moment we might get orders to hook in and continue the march. It was unlikely that we would be given such orders until the cool of the evening; but should some emergency make the step necessary, we would find ourselves in a pretty mess. Suzette had already realised the seriousness of the situation; out in the meadows, where men had thrown themselves down in the glaring sun, I could see her rousing them and helping them to get under cover. The great danger from the individual man's point of view, was that in his befuddled state he might wander away and be missing when we took up our march again.

What would follow would depend on each particular Tommy. If he had sense, when he found that he had lost his unit, he would report to the first British officer he encountered and get a written statement from the officer to that effect. Every day that he was absent, until he refound us, he would get a signed reference as to his movements. If, however, on coming out of his stupor he got frightened, he might hide himself; in which case, though he originally had no intention to desert, his action would be interpreted as desertion. Many a man has been court-martialed and condemned, when his only fault was stupidity and ignorance of military procedure.

You can't "crime" two-thirds of a battery; the only thing to be done was to take steps to avoid the consequences. I sent the guard to summon all the N.C.O.'s and officers to the horse-lines. We then brought together all the men who were still fit for duty and, having increased the guard, set to work to carry or lead all those who were incapable back to their quarters. When we had called the roll and knew that no one was absent, we made a search for any drink that might be concealed about the men's persons and then proceeded to sober up the worst cases by dashing buckets of water over them. When this had been done, we placed an armed guard at the entrance to every billet, with orders to permit no one to go out or to enter. We then left them to sleep it off.

At sundown a dispatch-rider dashed up to brigade headquarters. The sound of his motorbike chugging through the village had been sufficient warning to all the officers' messes; there were representatives from all the batteries waiting in the courtyard when the adjutant came out to give us the colonel's orders. "The orders are to hook in at once and be ready to move off by 9 p. m."

"In what direction?" we asked.

"I don't know," he said, "and that's no lie. The colonel doesn't know, but he's off to see the general. In any case we shan't be told until the last minute."

Then commenced the appalling job of getting a half-sober battery harnessed up, hooked in and looking sufficiently respectable that its true condition might not be apparent. This was a case when the iron discipline of the army showed at its best. A well-disciplined unit is never so drunk that it can't beat a teetotal one in which the discipline is lax. It was extraordinary how under the spur of necessity the men pulled themselves together; they had learnt how to make their insubordinate bodies obey their wills up front, flogging them forward to victory through mud and cold and weariness. With leaden eyes and shaking hands, they went through all the familiar motions, so that the battery was mounted and sitting to attention a quarter of an hour before the time appointed struck. In the inspection that followed, hardly a buckle was out of place or a piece of equipment ill-adjusted.

But there were some men who were kept hidden till the last moment—these were the dead drunk. It was our purpose to bring them out only at the last moment when, trusting to the gathering darkness to conceal their condition, we planned to bind them to the seats of the guns with drag-ropes. It takes all kinds to make an army; some who are the worst actors out at rest, are the finest heroes in action.

"There's those that does it because they're frightened." That thought kept running through my head as I searched the stern and haggard faces of these boys who had been shipped from the ends of the earth to die together. They didn't look the kind to be easily frightened. I knew they weren't the kind, for I'd seen them fighting forward through the mud-bath of the Somme and driving their guns into action through the death-traps of Farbus. But no one can guess rightly the agony which lies hidden behind the impassive masque of the external.

The sunset, lying low on the horizon, cut a brilliant line behind the shoulders of the drivers, causing their metal-work to glitter and emphasising the erectness of their soldierly bearing in the saddle. They looked a very different lot from the disorganised mob which eight hours earlier had lain scattered throughout the ditches of the countryside.

We were waiting for the major to arrive. He had gone to brigade headquarters with the other battery-commanders to receive final instructions from the colonel. As we waited the pool of darkness, which had at first washed shallowly about the gun-wheels and feet of horses, began to creep higher, till only the heads of the men and horses remained distinct against the frieze of the vanishing sunset—all else was vague and lost. A nightingale in a neighbouring thicket began to pour out its solitary song; far away in the intervals of silence a second bird answered. There was a heavy and yearning melancholy in what they said which played havoc with the accustomed stoicism of our hearts.

Suddenly along the road came the sound of a rider approaching at a rapid trot. The sharp tapping of the horse's hoofs changed to a dull thudding as he turned into the field. Then the thudding stopped. The major's voice rang out in an abrupt word of command, "Fall out the officers." From the various sections the officers galloped out and formed up before him in a half-circle.

"Take out your note-books and write down these names," he said; "they're the villages through which we shall pass on tonight's march. You will not tell any of the men the names of the villages and you'll burn your list in the morning. This information is only given to you in case some of the vehicles should break down, so that you may be able to bring them on to re-join the main party. And remember, absolute secrecy is necessary. Here are the names. Be careful with your flashlights as you write them down; keep them shaded. We don't want any Hun planes to get wind of us."

When we had replaced our note-books he nodded shortly, "That's all. In about five minutes we move off."

As I rejoined my section the number one of A. Sub rode up and saluted. "One of my men's missing, sir. He's Gunner Standish—a steady, quiet sort of lad: the chap as kept the gun in action single-handed, when all the rest of the crew was knocked out in the Willerval racket."

I remembered Standish well; I had had him in mind for the next promotion. He had won the Military Medal for his gallantry at Willerval, for fighting his gun alone, when the pit had become a shambles and all his comrades were lying about him, either wounded or dead. A fine piece of work, and especially fine for a chap of his nature, for he was nervous and high-strung,

84

and only seventeen, though in his keenness to enlist he had stated his military age as twenty.

I turned to the number one brusquely. "But you reported your subsection as complete a good half hour ago?"

"And it was complete then, sir. I spoke with the man myself. He slipped off while we was waiting for the major; he didn't ask no permission and didn't say a word to anyone."

"Perhaps he'd remembered that he'd left behind some of his kit. You'd better send someone after him at the double. Probably you'll find him in his billets."

"I've done that, sir, and he wasn't there."

"Had he been drinking?"

The sergeant shook his head. " It doesn't sound like Standish. He came of good people and was a trustworthy, well-conducted chap. He's never been up for office and was proud of it."

"Well," I said, "I'll have to report to the major, and then you and I will go and search for him. I'll wager we'll find him in his billets."

The major told me "Righto," and not to be long. We weren't running a kindergarten. If the chap got left behind, it was his own lookout.

As we hurried through the battery, they were carrying out the men who were incapable and lashing them with drag-ropes to the gun-seats like sacks. The billets were not more than a hundred and fifty yards from the horse-lines; they consisted of a mouldy stable, standing on one side of a farmyard, the whole of which was made foul by an accumulation of manure, as is the custom in French farmyards.

We tiptoed our way across the reeking mess, choosing our path so as not to sink too deeply into it. At the doorway to the low barn-like structure, we called the man's name, "Standish." When he did not answer, I loosened my flashlight from my belt and swept the ray along the broken floor and into the farthest corners. It seemed not unlikely that he might have fallen asleep there. All I saw was the refuse of worn-out equipment and empty bean-tins neatly gathered up into sacks. Already I could hear the first of the teams pulling out and the rattling of the guns on the road as they left the padded surface of the turf. If we did not hurry, we should be left behind ourselves.

"I told you he wasn't here, sir," the sergeant said.

Just as we were leaving, I flashed my light round the building for one last look. In so doing I tilted the lamp, so that the ray groped among the rafters of the roof. The sergeant started back with a curse, knocking the lamp from my hand. Just above his head he had seen it hanging, its face staring down at him crookedly.

We were too late when we cut him down; so we moved out that night upon our anonymous march with an extra passenger lashed to a gun-seat, on whose incapacity we had not counted.

The nightingales were still singing in the thickets when we left, singing of things forsaken, of beauty and of passion. I could not shake off the impression that it was their sweet, intolerable melancholy which had urged him to do it. If we had taken to the road an hour earlier, he would have been saved from that act. Poor lad ! He had played the game to the top of his bent, till he had passed the limit of his power to suffer. What was the limit of us who remained? How much further had we to go till we reached the breaking-point?

"There's those that does it because they're frightened." Trot-trot knew of what he was talking.

Chapter 13

On the Move Again

We march, and sleep, and work as in a dream. Nothing that we do or see seems any longer real to us. This inverted way of living by night and drowsing by day, blunts one's sense of actuality as with a drug. The only fact which remains constant is our ceaseless struggle against weariness.

There's no longer the faintest doubt as to where we are going; we're marching into the great shove, to which all the previous four years of war have been a preface. We're marching, if human endurance can carry us, straight into the heart of Germany. Among ourselves we make no more attempts to disguise what is intended; as though the doors of a furnace had been suddenly flung wide, we feel the heat of the trial which will consume us. Today is the fourth of August; we hope to be in Berlin by Christmas—some, but not all of us.

One looks curiously into the faces of his companions, half expecting to find their fates written on their foreheads. In so doing, he is not morbid; he simply braces himself to meet the facts of things which must surely happen. He knows that many of those who jest with him today, will lie endlessly asleep tomorrow. He wonders vaguely to which company he himself will belong—whether to the company of those who sleep or the company of those who go toiling forward. It seems as though those who are to fall in the battle must have been already selected; they must have been assigned some mark by which they may be detected. So one watches his comrades stealthily to discover the invisible tag which records their lot.

I find myself speaking to my men more as a friend and less as an officer; the thought of that last night-march, which all men must make solitarily, is drawing us together in a closer bond. A voice is continually whispering, "It may be the last time you can be decent to that chap—the last time."

I notice the counterpart of my own feeling in the attitude of the drivers towards their horses. They, too, realise that for many of us, whether human or four-footed, the hour of parting is approaching fast When stables are ended and the hungry crowd is dashing for the cook-house in a greedy endeavour to collar the biggest portions, the drivers turn back to their teams to give Chum and Blighty an extra pat and to shake the hay a little loose for them. The horses sniff against the men's shoulders and arch their necks to gaze after them with a mild wonder in their eyes.

In what part of the line lies the furnace into which they mean to hurl us? Some say that we are going to join up with the French—others that the Americans will be behind us and will leapfrog us when we have crumpled up the Hun front by our attack. There are many wild rumours, the most likely of which is that the neighbourhood of Rheims will be our jumping-off point. But to get us there they will have to entrain us; there are no signs of entraining at present. Nothing is certain, except that every night we are crawling southwards.

Are we brave or merely indifferent? The army crushes imagination and sentiment. To attain a certain object lives have to be expended—the more lives in proportion to the worth of the object. For those who plan the game at general headquarters death and courage are an impersonal sum in mathematics: so many men and horses in the field, of whom so many can be spared for corpses. But the sum is not impersonal for us. It consists of an infinite number of intimate computations: the little sums of what life means to us and of what our lives mean to the old men, mothers, wives, sweethearts who scan the casualty lists feverishly, hoping not to read our names among the fallen.

general headquarters cannot be expected to complicate their book-keeping by taking these bijou exercises in addition and subtraction into their immenser calculations.

For us, in its most heroic analysis, the arithmetic of war is an auditing of our characters—an impartial balancing of the selfish and the noble, the cowardly and courageous in our natures. Long ago when we first enlisted, before we had any knowledge of the horrors we were to suffer, we set ourselves on record as believing that there were principles of right and wrong at stake, in the defence of which it was worth our while to die. An offensive of this magnitude is the test as to whether, with an experienced knowledge of the horrors, we are still men enough to hold to our bargain and prove our sincerity with our blood. It is the test of scarlet the fiercest of all tests, which we encounter as heroes or avoid as moral bankrupts.

Yesterday, when the battery got drunk, there can be little doubt as to why it was done: the suspense of a judgement day for which no place or time had been allotted, made men afraid. Standish symbolises that terror. He could struggle with a fear which was present and which he could defeat with his hands, as he proved at Willerval; the fear, the coming of which was indefinite and the shadow of which groped only in his mind, crushed him. Perhaps the rest of us avoided his fate because we were of a coarser type. Maybe it was the very fineness of his mental qualities that tripped him up.

Whatever the difference, the fact remains that he failed in the test of scarlet; at the very moment when his comrades, equally weary, equally afraid, equally in love with life, were marching out to throttle the danger, he, poor lad, was dangling from a rafter, shameful and unsightly, a self-confessed quitter and pain-dodger. Why should a man do a thing like that? He rushed upon the certainty of death, when by living he would still have retained his chance of life. All through the war such incidents have happened, self-maimings, suicides, desertions—all manners of makeshift means of escaping the judgement day of the attack. But death is not to be avoided by running away from it; those who flee from it in the front-line find it waiting for them behind the lines at their comrades' hands. "I couldn't face the Huns," one deserter said with a kind of self-wonder, as he squared his shoulders bravely to meet the impact of the firing-squad, "but I can face this."

To my way of thinking it requires more courage to put a rope round your neck and fling yourself down from the rafters of a foul stable, or to hold yourself erect in the early dawn with your eyes blind-folded, waiting without whimpering for British bullets to strike you. There must be different kinds of courage, some of which war can employ and others—Cowardice gives one the courage of desperation, so that one can calmly perform the most terrible of acts. I suppose the explanation of such men as Standish is that terror, too long contemplated, drives them mad. How much longer can the rest of us stand its contemplation?

Last night's march was like a night of delirium with moments of consciousness; the moments of consciousness were the worst. We had scarcely struck the road before men started to fall asleep in their saddles. When orders to halt or to pull over to the right were passed down the column, they were not complied with. At first the horses saved us from tangles, for they heard the orders and, without guiding, carried them out. But then the horses commenced to sleep as they walked, adding to our danger the risk that they might stumble.

The entire battery was worn out and it was difficult to know on whom you could depend. We officers rode up and down, rousing the men and trying to keep the sergeants and corporals on the alert; but they, too, in many cases were no better and wandered nodding in their saddles. Soon after the last of the sunset had faded the night had become intensely dark; it was scarcely possible to see your hand before your face. Rain began to descend. The temperature sank and, after the heat of the August day, it became as cold as November.

Orders were passed back that every gunner and employed man had to walk that the vehicles might be lightened. Some of them had sore feet from the previous night's march; many of them were still groggy from their excesses. It required extraordinary vigilance to be sure that no one was falling behind and getting lost. We shuffled along under dripping trees in sullen silence. Very often our route lay by by-roads, that the traffic might be relieved on main thoroughfares. The by-roads were soggy and loose in their surface; branches and brambles slashed across our faces, leaping out on us from the dark.

Everything was on the move, tanks, heavies, siege-guns, transport. They were pushing south, all pouring in the same direction, and no one seemed to care whom he thrust aside so long as he himself got there. For long periods we were held up by lorries and caterpillars which had become ditched ahead of us. It seemed as though we could never reach our camping place before sunrise. Our strict orders were to be off the road and hidden before daylight. The men who had made themselves dead drunk before we started had the best of it; lashed to their gun-seats, they slept on blissfully unconscious of the rain and cold.

From midnight till dawn was the worst period; one's eyes were so heavy that it was an agony to keep them from closing. It became necessary to dismount and to lead one's horse to prevent oneself from drowsing. This remedy only brought new complications, for it was impossible to superintend one's section while on foot; mounted men in front who slept, kept colliding with the teams and vehicles. Everyone was cross, and strafing, and unjust by the time the day began to whiten. It had seemed that the sun had set for good; now that it had risen, we felt ashamed of our appearance. We were muddy and sodden; our one desire was to find a place where we could lie down and rest.

When we had limped into the field in which we are at present bivouacked, we found that only two teams could be watered at one time at the ford. This meant that grooming had to be prolonged until the last horse in the battery had been watered. By the time stables had been dismissed, the men were so tired that they did not care for breakfast, but tumbled off to sleep where they dropped.

Today I am orderly-dog, on duty for twenty-four hours from

reveille to reveille. I sit here among the bales of hay which have been thrown down from the G. S. wagons, and I watch—and I marvel, as I never cease to marvel, at the men's indomitable pluck. Now that they know what lies ahead of them, their behaviour is completely nonchalant and ordinary. They have accepted the idea of catastrophe and have dismissed it from their minds. If they refer to it at all, it is merely as material out of which to manufacture jokes against themselves.

Last night's march, with its cold and wet, being over is forgotten. More night-marches lie before them which may be worse than the last, but they cross no bridges until they come to them. For the moment the sun shines luxuriously and their fatigue is gone. Some of them are practising pitching with a base-ball; others are washing and cooling their swollen feet in the ford. The gramophone, which we always carry with us, is playing popular selections from the latest thing in musical comedy.

It's a point of honour with every officer in our mess when he goes on leave to bring back at least half-a-dozen new records. The tunes bring pleasant memories of girls and taxis and dinner-parties and dances, of crowded theatres jammed with cheering khaki, of uproarious laughter, of sirens blowing and bombs falling on London house-tops—the memories still are pleasant— and of late, adventurous home-comings along unlighted thoroughfares to sheeted beds. All of which memories are in rosy contrast to the stern laboriousness of our present.

Afar off I can see Bully Beef, toddling on chubby legs along the edge of the wood gathering wildflowers. That slim young soldier, who follows him with her eyes between intervals of mending a tunic, must be Suzette. The scene is extraordinarily restful. We might be planning to live forever. Wherever the eye rests the prevailing note is sanity and calm. And yet our calmness is only an outward pretence; it means nothing more than this, that we are in hiding from the spies of the enemy.

The woods which surround us were selected that no one might know that Foch's Pets are on the march. A further emphasis was laid on the magnitude of the ordeal which awaits us by an order regarding men under arrest, which we received this morning; they are to be released and the charges against them dropped, that they may be available for cannon- fodder. This is no act of mercy; it simply means that every last man will be needed for the replacing of casualties.

The true attitude of the fighting-man towards this concert-pitch commotion was expressed by the major, when he sat up in his sleeping-sack and rubbed his eyes at lunch-time. He looked an absurdly rebellious little figure in his khaki shirt-tails and without a tie or collar. "I tell you what it is; I'm fed up with all this secrecy and nonsense. I don't wonder that the chaps got drunk; when you're unconscious is the only time that you possess yourself. I don't mind the fighting; what I object to is this being mucked about by everybody. I'm not a major; I'm a policeman. And the colonels and generals who boss me, they're bigger policemen. In the army everyone who is not a Tommy is a policeman, with a stronger policeman above him to boss him. We interfere with one another to such an extent that we're disciplined out of our initiative and self-confidence. I'm sick of it all; I'm off."

He then explained in detail what it was he was sick of. He was sick of army-rations; sick of night-marches; sick of the paper-warfare which blew in from headquarters every hour of the day demanding answers; sick of having to strafe his men and being strafed in his turn by the colonel. He wanted to get away to where he didn't have to blow his nose in accordance with King's Regulations, where he didn't have to eat what a government had provided for him, where he didn't have to do everything in the dread of a calling down from higher authorities.

"You're orderly-dog for today," he said. "You can carry on. If you have to pull out, leave a mounted man behind to guide me on. I'm going to find a place where the food tastes different; if I find more than I want, I'll bring you back a portion. I'm going to take Captain Heming with me; the rest of the officers can wander about, so long as they get back by six o'clock and there are always two within call in the event of a movement order."

The rest of the officers are Tubby Grain, the centre section commander, Gus Edwine, the commander of the left section, Sam Bradley, who is in charge of the signallers, and Steve Hoadley, who is attached as spare-officer. Of them all I like Tubby best. He's fat, and brave, and humorous. He used to mix soft-drinks in a druggist's store, and started his career at the Front as a sergeant. He has a weakness for referring to himself as a "temporary gent" and, if he weren't so lazy, would make a cracking fine officer. He's as scrupulously honourable with men as he is unreliable with women. In his pocket-book he carries a cheap photograph signed, "Yours lovingly, Gertie."

He shows it to you sentimentally as "the picture of my girl," yet the next moment will recite all manner of escapades. His most permanent affair since he came to France is with an estaminet-keeper's daughter at Bruay. Out of the sale of intoxicants to British Tommies she has collected as her percentage a dot of fifty thousand *francs*—an immense sum to her. With this, when the war has been won and they are married, she proposes to buy a small hotel. Tubby is non-committal when she mentions marriage. I don't know how serious his intentions are, and I don't believe he knows himself. He gives her no definite answers, but writes her scores of letters. He gambles heavily and always loses; but whatever his losses, he's invariably cheery and willing to lend money. One has to take his companions as he finds them at the front; it's the kindness of Tubby's heart that recommends him.

Gus Edwine is of an entirely different stamp. He's conscientious, unmerry, and solid. He never plays cards, is poor company, but knows his work.

He has a girl who's a nursing-sister at a casualty clearing station. He takes his love with sad seriousness, and beats his way to her by stealing lifts on army lorries whenever we're within thirty miles of her hospital. I have my suspicions that that's where he's gone at present. He never tells. In a stiff fight he's a man to be relied on, and commands everyone's respect on account of his high morals and cool courage.

Sam Bradley is the only married officer in our battery. I don't think he can have been married long, for he smiles all the while quietly to himself as though he had a happy secret. Wherever we are, in a muddy dug-out or back at rest, the first piece of his possessions to be unpacked is a leather-framed portrait of a kind-looking girl. Much of his leisure is spent in writing letters, and most of his mail is in a round decided handwriting which we take to be hers.

Steve Hoadley is new to the war. He has never been in any important action and has yet to prove himself. He has a manner, which irritates the major, of "knowing it all," and is frequently in trouble. The men rather resent taking orders from him, since many of them have seen three years of active service. On the whole he does not have a happy lot. None of us have at first. He would get on all right if he wasn't so positive. I think he's made up his mind to seize this offensive to show his worth. Here's good luck to him in his effort.

Dan Turpin, the quartermaster—good old Dan with his large heart and immense sympathy for everybody—has just been to see me. He looked troubled as he halted in front of me, rubbing the wart on his nose thoughtfully.

"What is it, Quarter?" I asked. "Anything the matter with the transport? If it's a long story, you'd better take a pew while you tell me."

"It's nothing to do with the transport, sir," he said, and remained standing. "It's to do with what Suzette's doing over there."

"What is she doing?" I glanced lazily over the sunlit distance in her direction. "She's mending something, isn't she?"

Dan shook his head. Then, in order to give me another chance to guess, he added, "And it's got to do with what Bully Beef's doing."

"He's gathering wildflowers."

"Yes, He's gathering wildflowers," Dan said. "But she ain't mending anything; she's putting something together."

I unslung my glasses and focussed them to get a closer view.

"Ah, I see what she's up to now. She's made a kind of pillow out of a piece of horse-blanket and she's stuffing it with leaves."

"It's a pillow for his head," Dan said solemnly, "and the flowers is to cover him, before we throw the earth on."

Then I knew what Dan wanted and, rising to my feet, accompanied him without further words. In the wood, which surrounds our camp, we have just buried Standish, with Suzette's pillow beneath his head and Bully Beef's wildflowers for a covering. On account of the way he died, there was no parade of the battery to do him honour; but many of the men attended. Trottrot was there, whom everyone regards as untrustworthy under shell-fire. He was one of those who lowered the body, bruised by its last night's march on the gun-seat, into its narrow bed. While the short ceremony was in progress, the sound of the gramophone was stopped and the shouts of the base-ball pitchers died into silence. As we were seen to emerge from the wood, with scarcely a moment's delay, the sounds started up—not in callousness, but in a frenzied effort to forget. It was fully an hour after I had again seated myself among the bales of hay that I saw Suzette and Trottrot come back. I could guess what they had been doing—making the place beautiful. But why should Trottrot do that? He had not been the dead man's friend. Was it because he himself had come so near to cowardice that he could stoop to be tender?

I shall have no time to see what they have done to mark the grave, for a runner has just brought a movement order from brigade that we are to be prepared to march by sundown. It doesn't give us much of a margin, for the smoke-gray haze of evening is already creeping through the tree-tops. The major and Heming have not yet returned.

CHAPTER 14

Upsetting News

Last night we had another terrible march; neither the men nor the horses can stand much more of it. It isn't a matter of stoutness of heart; it's a plain question of physical endurance. How many more nights can men and horses go without sleep and bungle through the darkness of a strange country without collapsing? It isn't as though these were easy marches—all of them are forced. And then again, it isn't as though we had the knowledge that in a few days' time our present exertions would be followed by a rest; on the contrary, we know that our present exertions are as nothing compared with what will be demanded of us. Everybody is extraordinarily willing—there's no grumbling; but we're working under a high nervous tension of suspense which, in itself, is exhausting. If we were actually in battle, our excitement would carry us twice as far without letting us drop. In the presence of death one can achieve the incredible; these miracles are difficult to accomplish while one still has a reasonable certainty of living.

To tell the truth, our equipment isn't equal to the strain which is being laid upon it. Our teams are not matched; many of them are worn out; some of them consist of mules. One wonders whether they could go into action at the gallop without falling down. For the past three years there's been precious little galloping for the field artillery on the Western Front. Our work has consisted for the most part of dragging our guns up through mud at the crawl and afterwards of packing up ammunition on the horses' backs. This has broken the hearts of the animals, and robbed us of our dash and snap.

The animals which have been sent to us during the past two years to replace casualties are of an utterly inferior physique and stamp from those we had when war started. They're either ponies or draught-horses, or else patched-up, decrepit old-timers from the veterinary hospitals, which have been ill or wounded, and have been returned to active service to die in harness because no others are available. Our best animals are the few survivors we have of the original teams which we brought with us from Canada to France.

What is true of the horses is equally true of the men. The physical standard has dropped. In 1914, unless one were physically perfect, it was impossible to get accepted. Today both among the officers and in the ranks, one sees spectacled faces, narrow chests, stooping shoulders and weak legs. Boys and old gray-haired men go struggling up front through the mud today in France. Apparently, whatever his appearance, anyone is eligible to wear khaki who can tell a lie about how long he has been in the world.

I would make a guess that fully a third of our drivers and gunners had not seen their eighteenth birthdays at the time when their military age was recorded as twenty; on the other hand, there is a goodly proportion who are supposed to be thirty and are well over forty. And then, besides those who are too old or too young, there are the crocks—men who, like the horses from the veterinary-hospitals, have been patched up again and again and, after short rests at comfortless places somewhere between the base and the front-line, have once more been returned to active service to help push the Hun a little farther back before they themselves stumble into an open grave.

These crocks are for the most part men who have never had the luck to be wounded; if they had once reached a hospital in England, they would never have been allowed to see the front again. But the hospitals in France are compelled to be less merciful; their job is to repair the broken human mechanism and return it to the fighting-line so long as it has any usefulness.

Our crocks are chiefly men who have been crushed by exposure and hardship. They suffer from debility, poor feet, rheumatism, running-ears, etc.; the ear-troubles are caused by the sharp concussion of the guns in the pits when they are fired. I suppose those in authority have been forced to the opinion that all men are of equal value when they are dead, and that it's a waste of energy, when you're collecting material for cannon-fodder, to be too picksome.

In England, after the Hun drive of the spring had commenced, the magicians of the man-power boards were taking very much the same point of view, and arbitrarily improving the nation's health by raising re-examined C 3 men to an A 1 category. There are few men now, except the very aged, who are not on paper sufficiently healthy to die for their country. This changed attitude is summed up in the treatment of wounded men. Whereas to have been severely wounded was formerly a just reason for honourable discharge, today we have men still fighting who have made the trip to Blighty five times on a stretcher. There are officers who have suffered amputations, who are still carrying on.

Necessity knows no law; nevertheless, this desperate use which we are making of both human and four-footed material which is below par, makes itself felt when we are called upon for unusual efforts. We're beginning to fear lest before the show starts, these forced night marches may use up our reserves of strength. We do not own that there are any limitations to our power to obey and suffer, but common-sense tells us that there is a point beyond which the flesh cannot be driven, however great the heart.

Last night we were on the road from ten o'clock till seven this morning. It took two hours from the time when we pulled into our present place of hiding, till the men could lie down and rest. Very many of the horses had kicks and galls, all of which had to be attended to before anyone could think of himself.

I call this our place of hiding purposely, for it is so obviously just that. We are in a high rolling country, cut up into shadowy patterns by deep ravines, and dotted where it lies nearest the sky by squares and oblongs and triangles of woods. It is in one of these protecting woods that we have our bivouacs and horse-lines. We are so well covered from sight that peasants in the nearest village, two miles away, do not suspect our presence. We have not found it necessary to warn the men against revealing themselves; they're too played out to walk a yard further than is necessary.

A glance at the map makes our game of guess-work grow interesting. We're directly to the west of Amiens now; one night's march would bring us into the line. Amiens is the great junction-point of the railroad system which feeds the entire British Front and which connects us up with the French. The Hun came perilously near to capturing it this spring; since then it has been vacated by its civilian population and kept by the Hun continually under shell-fire.

The result has been that trains have had to make a detour by branch-lines to get round behind the Amiens salient, and our military transportation, as a consequence, has been working under a heavy handicap. Every fighting-man has been aware of this, for whereas formerly one could buy almost anything within in reason at the expeditionary force canteens, since the spring stocks have not been replenished and only limited quantities have been allowed to be purchased by each person.

There have been weeks together when one has had to scour the country far and wide to find a packet of cigarettes. After so much mystery and so many conjectures, it seems not unlikely that the push is to be put on to save Amiens.

The rumour concerning some Canadian troops having been sent to Ypres to deceive the Hun, was confirmed yesterday by our major. In his ride abroad he met the colonel of one of the battalions which had sent a detachment. From him he learnt that not only were Canadians and Australians sent over in a series of raids that they might be identified by the enemy, but that Canadian maple leaf badges and Australian slouch-hats had been issued to other units who were holding that line, that they might be mistaken for the storm-troops. Whether the ruse has succeeded in drawing the Hun reserves up north he could not learn.

The major and Captain Heming rejoined us last night just as I commenced to lead the battery out of the woods on to the high road. Directly I spoke to Heming I had the feeling that something was wrong; it was about half-an-hour later that the major sent back word for me to ride beside him and told me what had happened. It appears that at the officers' tea-room, where they had dinner, a number of week-old London dailies were strewn about. They sat glancing through them as they waited for the meal to be served. The major had got hold of a torn sheet, when he came across a column headed, *The Coldest Woman In London.*

"This sounds promising," he said to Heming; "I've met some of her sort myself."

Then he started to read the item aloud, throwing in his own racy comments. The coldest woman in London, it appeared, was a Mrs. Percy Dragott. She was reputed to have ruined many notable careers by her unresponsive attraction. She was extraordinarily beautiful and had been painted by many artists. The best known of all her portraits was one by ———.

"Hulloa, Heming, this can't be you, can it? A chap of your name is mentioned.——— By Jove, it must be you though; it says that this Heming was in Ottawa when war broke out, and is at present at the front with the Canadian artillery."

"Go on, sir, will you, if you don't mind? I'd like to hear a little more about this Mrs. Dragott."

That, according to the major, was all that Heming had said; but his face was very white, though his voice was hard and steady. So the major had no option but to read on. Mrs. Dragott's social eminence was recorded and hints were thrown out as to the personalities of the various prominent men who had broken themselves against her coldness. Her husband had committed suicide five years before, under circumstances which had helped to confirm her reputation for being a woman incapable of affection. And now, dramatically, after a hectic affair with a man who had proved to be already married, she had committed It was at this point that the paper was torn, leaving no clue as to what it was that she had done. Heming had been terribly upset, the major said, and had turned the place upside down to find the missing portion. " I have an idea," the major told me, "that Heming himself must have been fond of her."

"Perhaps," I said, and kept my mouth shut, for I remembered that Mrs. Percy Dragott was the name which Heming had handed to me that day on the Somme, when we were caught by the Hun out in No Man's Land and he had wriggled his way forward that he might risk his own life and save ours. What was it that she had done? Had she killed herself or the man? I could imagine all the questions that kept running through Heming's head, as he followed behind the wagon that carried Suzette, riding through the darkness at the rear of the column.

It only required a happening of this sort to bring home to us how much we are cut off from the outside world. Whatever tragedies are suffered by those whom we have loved, we cannot go to their help. Between them and us there is a great gulf fixed.

It's six o'clock in the evening. We had made up our minds that we would certainly be here for the night; it did not seem possible that, with men and horses so exhausted, they could send us on another march. That's what they're going to do, however. The harnessing up is nearly completed and the first of the teams are already being led out from the lines to the gun-park. A special order has just come in for me to join the colonel with a blanket and rations for twenty-four hours. I and one officer from each of the batteries are to be prepared to go forward with him in a lorry. Where we are going and for what purpose, we are left to surmise.

CHAPTER 9

Amiens

The adventure has begun in earnest. All the monotony of being foot-sore and tired is forgotten in this new excitement. They can push us as hard as they like; we shall not fail until our strength gives out. It's the game, the largeness and the splendour of it, that uplifts us. In the history of the world no fighting-men ever fought for such high stakes as those for which we are about to fight. Just as this war is out of all proportion titanic as compared with other wars which have been waged by men, so is this offensive, which we intend shall be the last and the decisive climax, out of all proportion titanic as compared with previous offensives.

It doesn't matter that we are physically inefficient for the task; we have been physically inefficient for other tasks, which we have nevertheless accomplished. We were sick, both men and horses, when we splashed our way furiously through the icy mud to those last attacks which won the battle of the Somme; none of us lay down on the job till we had been relieved in the line. The very day that we pulled out horses died in their tracks and men collapsed. We were like runners who had saved their last ounce for the final lap and had no strength left when they had broken the tape.

It will be like that again; stoutness of heart will carry us to success long after our bodies have backed down on us. From the first crack out of the box this is going to be a V. C. stunt for every man who takes part in it; that there won't be enough V. C's to go round doesn't trouble us. To have been privileged to share in such an undertaking will be reward enough and a sufficient decoration.

We're going to bust the Hun front so completely that it will never stand up again. We're going to make a hole in his defences through which all the troops which are behind us can rush like a deluge. We're going to achieve this end by the element of surprise and the devil-may-care ferocity of our attack. The effect will be like the breaking of a dam: we shall spread and spread till the military arrogance of Germany is flooded out of sight and only the steeples and roofs of the highest houses show up above the ruin's surface to mark the spots where the ancient menace was trapped and drowned.

Last night we found our lorries waiting for us at a cross-roads; they were headed in the direction of the road which was marked "To Amiens." The sun was sinking behind the uplands as we set out; the last sight we had as we looked back through the golden solitude was our brigade of artillery slowly winding like a black snake out of the wood and losing itself in a fold of the hills. The colonel was silent; he gave us no information, save that we were going forward to choose battery positions and alternative routes for bringing in our guns and ammunition in case some of the routes were shelled. For the rest, we conjectured that the lorries were taking us past points where it would not be wise for the brigade to travel.

We had not been going long, when we began to pass Australian infantry. First of all we met them in isolated groups, strolling down the lanes and through the wheat, two and two, with their arms about the waists of peasant-girls. Very often the girls had plucked wildflowers for their lovers, and had stuck them in the button-holes of their tunics or had pinned them against the brims of their broad slouch-hats. One wondered with how many soldier-men these girls had walked since the war had started, and how many of their soldier-men still remained above ground to kiss the lips of a living girl.

Without being told, there was something of false flippancy

and yearning in their attitude which made us understand that these lovers for a moment were taking their last stroll together. Like the Canadians, they are storm-troops, and will be lost in the smoke of battle before many days are out.

At a turn in the road we came across a girl who had flung herself down beside the hedge and was sobbing with her face buried in her hands. Farther on, by a few hundred yards, we passed a boy-private, who kept halting and glancing back with trouble in his eyes, and then again making up his mind to go forward. Many a deserter has been shot not because he was a coward, but because he had grown too fond of a girl.

We entered a village where all was in commotion.

The dusk had fallen. In the windows lights glimmered. Trumpets were sounding. Across farmyards, and in and out of barns men hurried with lanterns. Infantry, in their full marching order, were tumbling out from houses and forming up, two deep, along the street. Rolls were being called and absentees searched for. Officers on horseback fidgeted impatiently or went at the sharp trot, carrying messages. Bursts of laughter and song from the gardens behind the cottages, seemed to mock the atmosphere of military sternness. Behind the darkness there was the knowledge of stolen kisses. The storm-troops were saying "Goodbye" to life and moving one stage nearer to the slaughter. We won free from the village and were soon on a high road, doing our forty miles an hour.

In the dusk the sharp details of the country were blurred, but we saw enough to know that its aspect was changing. There were no more peasant-girls with their soldier-lovers; the fields were uncared for—all the civilian population had been pushed back. We came to villages full of deserted houses, with roofs smashed and walls gaping where bombs had been dropped. Under the protection of trees, in lanes and side-roads, motor and horse-transport was waiting for the sky to become sufficiently dark for it to be safe for them to advance. At every crossroad we were halted by military-police till our special order had been presented and examined. Ahead of us the cathedral spires and towers of Amiens grew up; like fire-flies flickering above them, though actually at a distance of miles behind them, the flares and rockets of the Hun Front commenced their maniac dance.

We crept into the city, slowing down to avoid gaping holes in the pave. It was a city of the dead. No movement was allowed till night had grown completely dark. Shutters sagged on their hinges. Doors stood wide, just as they had been left in the hurry of the exit. Windows stared blindly, with broken panes and curtains faded and flapping. On the pavement the debris lay strewn of household furniture which had been carefully carried out, and then left in the mad stampede of the panic. One could picture it all as the terror had spread and the horror had been whispered from mouth to mouth, "He's broken through—the Boche is coming."

Amiens, as I last saw it, was the front-line's dream of Paradise—a place where one could keep warm, where one could wash to his heart's content, where one could laugh and live without being hungry, where one could hear the voices of children and watch the faces of pretty girls. It was a city of clubs, tea-rooms, cinemas, canteens, tramways, hotels, hospitable fires.

In Amiens one could still believe in the glory of war, for the Indian cavalry with their brilliant turbans and the hunting-men from the Home Counties were there, all waiting for the break in the line to occur when the swordsmen of the Empire would get their chance. It was more honestly gay than Paris, more gallantly mad than London, more wistful and unwise than either. From in front of Courcelette, where one drowned in the mud, it was possible to reach Amiens by lorry in a handful of hours. Amiens was to us, when I last saw it, a glimpse of Blighty set down at the back-door of hell.

But since then the Hun drive of the spring had occurred and, with the approach of tragedy, every vestige of gallantry had vanished. War, with its inevitable squalor, had laid hands on everything, revealing itself in its true colours. Like mutilated human faces, the fronts of houses hung in tatters, indecently displaying all those intimate secrets of family life that the kindly walls had hidden. Shells had fallen; bombs had been dropped. Even as we entered, we could hear the angry roar of detonations. Dead men sprawled about the streets, twisted by the anguish of their final struggle. Dogs and cats, of appalling leanness, slunk in and out the ruins.

As we passed the station, with its great span of girders, a shell crashed through with a splash of glass. It was a city through which demented solitude wandered. We hurried on. An ambulance lurched by us, returning from the front, and halted by an emergency hospital. We had a glimpse of the stretchers being carried underground into the temporary security of the cellars. Overhead the fierce *rat-a-tat* of machine-guns commenced, where two fighting-planes circled in mid-air. Someone shouted to us to put out our cigarettes; after that there was no smoking.

Danger is like strong wine; it drives out weariness. While our lives were secure, those long night-marches had seemed an intolerable hardship. Now that death was present, the entire manhood in us stiffened to fight off the peril. Mere weariness was forgotten—a good night's rest could cure that; but if once death should get the upper-hand, there was no kindliness of human skill that could restore us. Our spirits rose as we drew nearer to the horror of the carnage. There is something wonderfully stimulating about terror; the challenge of it makes one forget his body. That night as we sped through Amiens and during all the days and nights that followed, it seemed more as if we were hunting death than as if death were hounding us.

We had left the cathedral far behind. Whenever we looked back, so long as any light was in the sky, we could see it standing dark and brooding against the horizon. We had by now travelled off the maps in our possession, by means of which we had been following our journey. The colonel, seated beside the driver of the leading lorry, gave him his directions. He alone was aware of where we were going. But we knew by the wholesale demolition that this was one of the main national roads which had been most fiercely contested in the spring fighting, before the headlong rush of the Hun had been stopped. The tracks of the railroad, which paralleled it, had been torn from their bed. Bridges had been blown up. Improvised forts had been constructed in hollows where an advance could be checked by machine-gun fire.

In my memory vivid descriptions recurred of the stubborn resistance which our men had put up. They had retreated and retreated, overpowered by weight of numbers. They had been deprived of water and food and sleep, and still they had fought on. Their officers had been killed; their N. C. O.s were gone; they had lost touch with their units, and yet they had never lost their sense of conquest—they dug their toes in and fought on.

Along this very road they had crawled on hands and knees when they could no longer walk; but they had crawled backwards, with their faces always towards the enemy, who followed them staggering drunkenly in his steps from exhaustion. There were German battalions which had marched forty miles at a stretch, only to be shot down by these broken Tommies who never knew when they were beaten. As the agony of the spring became more and more obvious a cold anger grew in our hearts. We were going to revenge that mud-stained mob who ought to have been beaten, but had won by their own invincible doggedness. From graves in the darkness the anonymous dead watched us pass.

We were travelling more slowly now; the road was becoming congested with transport and with batteries pulling into action. From lanes and cross-country routes which avoided Amiens, they began to pour into this main artery of traffic. Fully two-thirds of the transport consisted of motor-lorries, bringing up ammunition to the various dumps which were being established in rear of the point where the blow was to be struck. We crept along without lights of any kind, speaking to each other in whispers lest the Hun should become aware of the commotion of our progress.

By day all this country had appeared to be naked and nothing had been seen to stir. The moment night had gathered every road and lane had become as dense with traffic as Piccadilly Circus at the theatre hour. One wondered where so much energy had concealed itself, and marvelled at the army organization which knew to within a hundred yards where each separate group of energy could be found.

Behind these speculations and imaginings lay a graver thought—the thought of all the men, horses and engines of war which had been pouring eastward for four years, only to dash themselves to pulp and blood, and to sink from sight in the debatable quagmire which separates the hostile armies. Where had so many come from? How much longer could the stream be kept flowing? Above our heads, like invisible trains slowing down as they neared their destination, the long range shells of the Huns roared and lumbered, and almost halted before they plunged screaming among the sullen roofs of Amiens.

During the last part of the journey I nodded. It was midnight when I was awakened by the stir of my companions climbing out. "We're here," someone said. Where here was none of us knew; for the time being we were too sleepy to care. Everything was in total darkness; it was impossible to see more than a yard ahead. The air was stealthy with the muffled breathing of an immense crowd.

You held out your hand to guide yourself and found it touching the leg of a mounted man. Then, as our eyes became accustomed to the blackness, we found that we were in a village street, packed with two streams of traffic, the one going up to the front loaded, the other returning empty. We listened to the whispered orders—some were in English, but many were in French. So the French were going to be behind us!

Not a light was to be seen anywhere. Someone struck a match to start a cigarette; immediately, almost before the flame had burst, came the angry order, "Put that light out." The windows of the houses were all dead; but if one pressed against them, he could hear voices and knew that behind the heavy curtains drawn across them men bent over tables and worked beneath shaded lamps. Carrying our blankets and rations, we wormed our way in single file through the traffic, entered a court-yard and found ourselves in a partially destroyed house. There were two rooms, mildewed with damp, bare of furniture and littered with the debris of the last soldiers who had been billeted there. By the broken equipment that they had left, we knew that they had been French.

After waiting for about a quarter of an hour we were joined by the colonel, who brought with him an armful of maps. We wedged up the windows with sacking and then lit a candle.

"Everyone will know by tomorrow," he said, "so I may as well tell you now. We're going to pull off the stunt for which we've been training all summer. We believe that we've got the Hun guessing; he doesn't know where we are. By marching only at night and camping in woods by day, we've thrown him off our track. He knows that something is going to be pulled off and he's restless; but he doesn't suspect us in this part of the line— he's looking for us further north.

"That he is still kept in ignorance must be the aim of every man and officer. Success depends on it. Our job is just this. On August 8th at dawn we attack. That gives us three days to make all our preparations. The work of building the gun-platforms and stocking the positions with ammunition must be carried on only by night. By day everything must be quiet—any un-usual movement would give away all our plans. The enemy has the high ground; he can look directly down on us. We're taking over from the French, so if the enemy sees khaki uniforms in this part of the line instead of blue-gray, he'll know at once what to expect.

"We shan't drag our guns into position until the night be-fore the show commences. We shan't register them—we shall get them on for line with instruments; so the first shot we fire will be in the attack and the first knowledge he has that there's a concentration of artillery in this area will be at the identical moment when our infantry are advancing behind the tanks. By that time he'll know too late; we shall have captured his de-fences. There's only one other thing I want to say before we get to work on details: the positions which have been allotted to us are so exposed that he can look almost down the muzzles of our guns. Any tracks made on the turf will give us away; even if they've escaped his observers, they'll show up on his aero-plane photographs. You must camouflage your ammunition with the greatest care, making use of natural camouflage to the greatest extent, such as ditches, wheat-fields and the shadows of trees. If once your positions are discovered, they'll become murder holes for everyone concerned.

"And now for the positions themselves; in less than three hours we go forward to inspect them. I want each of you to choose one main position and an alternative one which you can take up in case you're shelled out of the first. When you've settled upon your positions I want you to reconnoitre every possible route in. It's nearly one now; we shall have to leave here in two hours. We've got to do all our work between dawn and when the morning mist rises. Meanwhile here's a map apiece, which I should advise you to study, so that you may have some idea of the country. You'll have to carry the idea in your heads; no flash-lamps will be allowed. Our brigade is going to sit astride the road which runs along the ridge from the Gentelles Woods to Domart. The general plan of strategy is to take the Hun by surprise and tumble him back—and so save Amiens. After that our game is to sail out into the blue and penetrate as far as we can."

"To sail out into the blue and penetrate as far as we can." As long as the war has been going we have dreamt of that. Out in the blue one takes a sporting chance and, if the worst happens, goes west in clean fields and beneath an open sky. In the trenches one dies like a trapped rat, amid filth and corruption, nailed beneath a barrage. In the trenches men are so crowded that they lose their personalities; they kill and are killed in the mass. Out in the blue it's a man to man fight, in which individual cunning and valour count. Long after the colonel had left us and the candle had been blown out, we lay in our blankets and whispered of what "into the blue" might bring to us in the way of adventures.

111

By three o'clock we were on the road, shivering in the raw night air. The traffic was all going in one direction now and consisted for the most part of ammunition-limbers returning empty to their wagon-lines. About a mile out of the village we swung off to the left, travelling across country to where the eastern point of the Gentelles Woods showed shadowy against the sky. The going was rough and the night so black that it was difficult to see where one's feet were treading. Several times we blundered into wire and stumbled into partly filled trenches. We had no one who had been over the ground to guide us, so had to rely for our direction on our memories of the maps. At the Gentelles Woods we struck the high road, which runs along the ridge between pollarded trees straight down to Domart and the Hun front-line.

The sheer audacity of the offensive, as planned, took away our breath when we saw the nature of the landscape. It was a great plateau, lacking in any cover and scored by deep ravines to right and left; every inch of it was commanded by the enemy's higher ground. The road along the ridge was a direct enfilade for the enemy; the air was heavy with decaying flesh and the sickening smell of explosives. It ran level for fifteen hundred yards, then it began to dip down to Domart, which lay in a valley which crossed the road at right angles. The near side of the valley was in our hands; the far side, which rose to a much greater height, was in the enemy's. To attempt to bring artillery into that area, especially when all the work had to be carried on by night, and to expect to be able to do it unobserved, seemed madness.

Shells were coming over far too frequently for comfort; the enemy was searching and sweeping the Gentelles Woods, so we set out at a smart walk along the ridge in a south-easterly direction.

CHAPTER 16

To the Orchard

One by one our party left us, turning off alongside-roads to search for the particular map-locations which had been suggested as positions for their batteries. At last only I and one other officer, named Strong, remained together. The spot for which we were looking was an orchard to the right of the road along the ridge which we were travelling. We walked on and on. It seemed an inter-minable distance. A fine rain began to descend, which had the effect of mist, blurring the few land-marks which one could still identify as though a muslin curtain had been drawn across them.

Every now and then the humpy figure of a man with a ground-sheet flung over his rifle and shoulders, would loom up out of the dark and pass us. It seemed as though he was always the same man, working like a beast of prey round and round us in circles, waiting for us to drop. We spoke to him several times, but he never deigned to answer. Men rarely answer when they are spoken to on the road up front at night. Whether it is that they enjoy the luxury which darkness affords them of not recognising authority, or that the sullenness of night has entered into their souls, or that they are afraid of being delayed one extra minute from the much needed sleep which awaits them in some wretched kennel, I do not know.

But the effect of this silence on anyone who is travelling a country with which he is unfamiliar, is to arouse the suspicion that he may, unwittingly, have gone too far and have wandered behind the enemy's line. This has happened quite often. Many an officer has started out on a night reconnaissance and disappeared as completely as if the ground had swallowed him up. In some cases the next news has been from a prisoners' camp in Germany. In others a spy has been captured wearing his uniform; the presumption has been that he was murdered by a Hun agent on our side of the line and that his body has been tossed into some lonely shell-hole. On account of this danger no man or officer is allowed to go unaccompanied within two miles of the front—a rule which is invariably broken.

We had walked so far that we had begun to think that we had passed our orchard, when quite suddenly we stumbled across it. It consisted of about a hundred trees. The first position lay behind the orchard in a wheat-field; the second in front, strung out along a dyke, with the whole of the Hun country staring at it. From every theoretical point of view the first position was the better, as the trees afforded it a certain amount of cover; on the other hand it had the disadvantage of being too obviously a good gun-position.

If the Hun were to study his map for a likely place to shell a battery, he would be sure to pick on the rear of the orchard. The position was too ideal to be safe. Experience has proved that a bad position is often more healthy in the long run. It can be so damned bad that it's almost good. The enemy would scarcely believe that any battery-commander would be fool enough to select it. Another disadvantage of the first position was that the wheat, while it would hide the guns, might easily be set on fire and be converted from a protection into a trap.

Strong and I tossed for the choice; when I won, rather to his amazement I chose the bad position in front of the orchard. How bad it was I had not realized till the dawn began to rise. Then I discovered that the muzzles of our guns would poke out straight across the valley. The road, from the Gentelles Woods to Domart, skirted the left of the position, dipped down into the valley across No Man's Land and climbed the further slope by a mass of trees, marked on the map as Dodo Wood. From Dodo

Wood the enemy could have watched a cat washing itself on the ground where our guns were to come into action.

One false step and the entire position could be wiped out. On the other hand, if we could contrive to lie doggo until the show commenced, the smoke of battle would confuse an enemy observer, so that he would be likely to mistake our flash for the flash of the battery in the wheatfield behind the orchard—in which case it would be they and not we who would be knocked out. That was the gamble one had to take. If one guessed wrong, he brought down death on most of his chaps.

As day commenced to whiten, it became unwise to hang about in so exposed a place. All the transport that had creaked and thundered through the night, had vanished from sight and sound for over an hour. Under the sickly pallor which was spreading through the sky, the landscape looked afraid and haggard. One saw now for the first time how horribly it had been battered. Not a tree on the road along the ridge had escaped; they tottered like old prize-fighters too proud to run away, with their arms drooping by their sides, waiting for the knock-out blow to fell them.

The rain had ceased, the smell of death was in the air. The ground seemed soaked with men who had died. Mingled with this smell was the sickly sweetness of gas and the suffocating fumes of explosives. The blanket of mist which had made us safe, was breaking up and drifting away in little ghostly clouds. It was the hour when the gunners on either side of No Man's Land stand down on their harassing fire and wait breathlessly for the S. O. S. which betokens an attack. When that comes, they open up at an intense rate of fire, four rounds per gun per minute. To be caught in such a hail-storm of destruction is not pleasant, and especially unpleasant when you know that you are serving no good purpose by your presence. We gazed behind us at the Gentelles Woods; the shells had ceased to burst and all was quiet. "Let's make our getaway while the going is good," Strong said.

Crouching and running low along the ground, we scrambled through the orchard and plunged into the wheatfield. In order that we might reconnoitre a new route of approach to the positions, we struck off to the left, entering a ravine which led down to a lower road which paralleled the shell-torn highway along the ridge. From a distance the ravine looked wild and forsaken; not a plume of smoke rose; nothing stirred.

As we walked down it, we discovered that what we had mistaken for rocks and patches of brush, were actually carefully camouflaged ammunition-dumps and battery positions. Not only this ravine, but every hill and slope was stiff with guns of every calibre, lying masked and silent, waiting for the great hour to strike when they would blow the Hun out of his strongholds. In rabbit-warrens dug far down beneath the surface, the French artillery-men bided their time. Some of them peeped out to watch us pass, with eyes uninterested and fatalistic.

Our idea of the scope of the attack which was planned grew as we investigated further. We also began to get a picture of what these preparations had already cost in lives. Horses and men lay strewn about in every stage of decomposition. Some had only been dead for hours; others were the skeletons of those who had fallen in the fierce counter-drive, which had halted the Huns' rush towards Amiens. One wondered how that rush had ever been halted and, when it had been halted, how the line had been held. Every bit of high ground in our hands was over-topped by a higher point in the hands of the enemy. From all directions on the eastern horizon, from woods and coppices in a great semi-circle, the Hun gazed down; it was impossible to avoid his eyes. Every now and then a scurry of bullets or a whizz-bang bursting near us would remind us of this fact, and we would flatten ourselves.

It took us two hours to regain the town from which we had started where, by pre-arrangement, we were to make our reports to the colonel. From him we learnt that our batteries had marched in during the night and had set up their horse-lines in the Boves Woods. That these woods should have been chosen for our camp was the crowning stroke of audacity; how audacious we did not realise until we saw the camp itself.

All the woods of this district are on hill-tops, the slopes of the valleys and the valleys themselves being cleared for agriculture; it is therefore a very difficult country in which to hide from the planes of the enemy. Infantry can keep out of sight in the villages and towns, taking their chances of shell-fire and digging themselves in beneath the houses. But the horse-lines of mounted troops are unmistakable when seen from the air, and almost impossible to disguise. To take to the woods was our only choice. The enemy was aware of this; he bombed every cluster of trees as soon as night had fallen, and raked them both day and night with shell-fire.

The Boves Woods lay behind the town. To reach them it was necessary to climb a bald ascent of chalk, almost incandescently white, and to cross a plateau which was as open and conspicuous as a parade-ground. In the old days of hand-to-hand fighting and cavalry charges the height must have been well-nigh impregnable. In general formation it was not unlike the Heights of Abraham, even to having a river for its defence, which wound about its foot. The ascent, the *plateau* and the woods were full in sight of the enemy on their eastward side. To select such a landmark for one's horse-lines was the last word in foolhardiness. A water-cart wandering out on to the *plateau* in full daylight would have given the secret away. Had the enemy once started shelling, he would have discovered all that was necessary to make public the attack.

The night-marches, the decoys sent up to Ypres, the whole web of strategy, the object of which was to make him muster his reserves opposite to the most remote part of the line, would all have proved useless. In choosing the Boves Woods as our place of hiding we were staking our own foolishness against the enemy's commonsense; he would never credit us with being so reckless. We were attempting to defeat his cleverness by our own seeming stupidity. Our chance of getting away with such a trick was one in a thousand. In the choice of our gun-positions and in all that we were attempting, it was on the thousandth chance that we were gambling.

On leaving the colonel, since it was daylight, we had to work our way round the hill and approach our camp from the westward slope. We found that the town had been badly hammered, and except for the troops who hid like rats beneath the fallen roofs, was entirely deserted. We found also that a river which wandered through it, cut it in two, and was crossed by a single bridge, which was quite incapable of taking all the traffic. This bridge had to be shared by both ourselves and the French, and had evidently been responsible for the delays and congestions which we had noticed on the night of our arrival. One wondered what would happen if the attack failed, and a retreat became necessary. How could we get the guns away across a single bridge which the enemy would certainly keep under fire? It was plain that failure and retreat had not entered into the vision of our present strategy. It was neck or nothing. We were staking our all on success.

At the entrance to the woods Strong and I parted company and went in search of our respective batteries. The undergrowth was drenched and had been trampled into boggy lanes where the horses had been led down to water. Everything was dark and dank. The overhead foliage was so dense that heat and light never permeated. A cathedral dusk and chill mounted from the roots of the trees to the topmost branches. Distantly, at the end of the long aisles of trunks, the day shone like stained-glass windows.

I had to hunt for some time before I found my unit. The place was packed with weary horses and sleeping men. At last I came across them, the horses tethered to ropes stretched between the wheels of the limbers, and the men rolled in blankets, mud-splashed and motionless. Everything was so still that I might have stumbled across a refuge of the dead. There were no fires burning; without being told, I knew that fires were not allowed. We might be storm-troops, but we looked neither triumphant nor terrible.

Beneath a stretch of canvas I espied my sleeping-sack. Without more ado, removing my boots and tunic, I tumbled into bed.

My last conscious thought was of the gun-position, with Dodo Wood glaring down at it. Would it have been better to have chosen the other position behind the orchard?

CHAPTER 17

Preparing For the Attack

This the last day; tomorrow at dawn we attack. We are still lying hidden in the Boves Woods; though other woods to the rear of us have been bombed and harassed, no shell has fallen here as yet. The enemy doubtless watches this wood for the flash of the guns and, having seen none, has not thought it worth his while to waste ammunition upon it. Our foolhardiness in camping directly under his eyes has certainly paid us, for there is scarcely any other place where we would not have suffered casualties.

It's afternoon; beyond the dim cavernous shadow of these trees the hot August sun is shining. The white chalky hills gleam molten and dazzle one's eyes with their glare. The valleys, which spread away for miles below us, float tethered in the hazy air. Everything looks tranquil and dreamlike; it is difficult to believe in our own reality and in the reality of our monstrous purpose. Surely we shall wake up to find ourselves safe at home and to laugh at our fantastic imagining that we are soldiers.

Yet within a handful of hours all this peacefulness will vanish; the mask of summer quiet will be torn aside and every ridge and rock will belch fire and destruction. The French have dragged their guns into the most daringly inaccessible places; there they lie basking in the fragrance of wild thyme with all the world below them, their muzzles pointed towards the stolen country, waiting for the hour of reckoning to strike.

Our men were advised to rest this afternoon and to get as much sleep as possible; but already the fever of excitement is in their blood. Many of them have gone down behind the hill to bathe and are washing their clothes in the river. One of the amazing spectacles of our place of hiding is the impassive aspect of the eastern slope as compared with the stirring life which goes on on its western side.

All our preparations are completed; there is nothing more that can be done until darkness has gathered. It was on the morning of August 5th that the battery marched into those woods. The following night was spent in carrying up ammunition and sand-bags to the gun-position. We hid them in ditches on either side of the Gentelles-Domart Road and beneath the trees of the orchard. Last night we completed the stocking of the position with ammunition and dragged in the guns. The guns we also hid in the orchard, covering them with branches to break up their outline, so that they might not arouse suspicion in the mind of the enemy.

The work was very exhausting and slow on account of the congestion of the traffic. The return from the Derby was nothing to it. It was like being caught in the procession of the Lord Mayor's Show. In the case of a break-down in front, it was impossible to swing out and get forward. Men stood elbow to elbow and vehicles hub to hub. Limbers and led animals were packed solid, the one stream moving up and the other returning. In order to get the work done every horse and man had to make at least two journeys. The main ammunition-dumps, at which the limbers were loaded, were from two to three miles away; when one had been emptied another had to be located in the darkness. To forward-positions, such as ours, there are only two highways of approach—the road along the ridge and the road along the valley; the Hun keeps the ridge-road continually under harassing fire. If a team was ditched or struck, it meant that every battery for a mile back was held up.

The worst cause of delay was the single bridge across the river. Most of our confusion arose from the fact that the roads were used by both French and British troops, and were controlled by military-police of both nations. If a British Tommy wished to disobey a French traffic-control, he had ample excuse in pretending not to understand his language. The result was that the two streams, coming and going, often got wedged and double-banked. Everyone was working under a nervous tension. His own job was all important to him. It had to be accomplished between dusk and sunrise. If he failed, no matter what the delays, no excuse would be taken by superior officers.

The consequence was a wild hustle and scramble, all of which took place under the cover of darkness There were only two nights in which everything had to be done. Our orders were that on the night previous to the attack, which is tonight, the roads were to be left free from wheel-traffic for the infantry and the tanks. The tanks are being brought in at the last moment to go over the top ahead of the attacking troops and to trample down the enemy's defensive wire. The cutting of the wire is usually done by special artillery-shoots, which of course announce to the enemy something boisterous in the near future. But on this occasion we are doing no announcing, so the tanks have to perform the task which formerly fell to the artillery. Their job is to plunge their noses into our barrage and stamp a path through all obstacles that would impede our infantry.

If one survives this war, will it seem more real in retrospect than it does now? Now it seems a wild distorted dream from which we shall awake presently. The memory of these last two nights seem the ramblings of a disordered mind. The very air was acrid with the sweat of men and horses driven beyond their strength. You heard and smelt them floundering in the darkness, but you rarely saw or felt them. They went by you breathing hard and indistinct as shadows. You heard men swearing in English and in French—swearing as passionlessly and mechanically as one who repeats a remembered prayer, and through all the agony without intentional blasphemy recurred the name of Christ.

Above our heads we could hear the purring of hostile planes. Every now and then a bomb dropped and the earth rose up to meet it flaming red. For a moment the country for miles round was ensanguined and we saw one another distinctly, frightened horses rearing, riders in steel helmets crouching low in their saddles and men hanging on to the bridles to hold the horses down. Then the flame failed, like a torch stamped out, and we heard nothing but sobbing breath. While on the road the fear was always with us that at any minute our doings might be discovered and the enemy might open fire. If he had, few would have escaped.

Quite remarkably he still seems totally ignorant of what is planned. One would have supposed that the roar of so much travel, always springing up at night and dying down with the dawn, would have warned him. We can hear it ourselves, even though we are part of it. It sounds like the muffled beat of many drums, accompanied by the shuffling of an immense crowd. It commences very distantly from miles back as the dusk begins to settle, and swells and swells in volume throughout the night, receding and finally dying into silence as the dawn spreads and the sun begins to rise. If the enemy knows or suspects, he is waiting to catch us the night before the attack—tonight—when with so many men crowded into one area he can deluge us with death. That may be his game, but according to our information he is still puzzled as to our whereabouts.

Our job tonight will be the heaviest we have tackled. We set out on foot as soon as the day begins to fail, taking with us the gun-crews, the signallers and a fatigue-party with sandbags, picks and shovels. The work before us consists of digging gun-platforms and throwing up some kind of protection for the gunners, of man-handling the guns into position and getting them on for line, and of sorting out the shells and carrying them to immediately in the rear of the gun-platforms. We have not yet been told the exact hour at which the show opens, but we know that all our preparations for opening fire must be completed by 4 a. m.

The inconsideration which we have to show for our men fills me with shame. We have to work them as if they were in bondage. If we have to treat them remorselessly, we get no better treatment ourselves. In the army every man in authority is a slave-driver and himself, in turn, a slave. The more one does, the more he may do; in the ranks, where the greatest sacrifices are made, there are few rewards and precious little thanks. One smiles out here when he reads of strikes at home for shorter hours and higher rates of pay. Our pay is a mere pittance, which does not pretend to be approximately equivalent to the service rendered. Our hours are as long as the authorities who control our destinies like.

For the last five nights our men have marched and worked incessantly; during the day they have been able to get no proper rest, what with the constant interruptions caused by stable-parades, guard-mountings, fatigues and pickets. Tonight will be the sixth night that they have gone without sleep; at dawn they have to face up to the strain of battle, showing coolness, courage and steadiness of nerve.

The standard we demand of ordinary men is too heroic, especially when we treat their sufferings as of no consequence. And yet these perfectly ordinary men, bully-ragged by discipline, disrespected in their persons, handicapped by hard-ship and abused in their strength, rise unfailingly to heights of nobility whenever the occasion presents itself. What is more, they do it utterly unconsciously, with the careless untheatric grandeur of original men.

The army and its steam-roller methods have done much to degrade their external appearance, but they have not been able to destroy the secret glory which made them willing to submit to the rigors and indignities of the scarlet test. They are out here to prove their manhood. They came here to die that the world might be better. The army chooses to regard such courage as natural—so natural that it is almost to be despised; but it cannot make them lose their elation and quiet gladness in their sacrifice.

Suzette! My thoughts are forever turning to her—she impersonates the fineness for which we die. She moves among us with her patient serving hands and her quiet self-forgetting kindness.

After all, our test—the test which we are called upon to face tomorrow—is the test which women have been facing without complaining throughout the ages, giving up their bodies to be smashed, that by the birth of a new life the world may start afresh. The battlefields on which her sisters have fallen lie far and wide, wherever men have trodden and still tread. For her and her sisters the test of scarlet is never ended. Perhaps it is because of this that she follows us and understands.

It's time for evening-stables; the men are waking up and crawling out from the underbrush with blinking eyes. The chaps who are to go forward with us to fight the guns are already at the cook-house, getting their supper. They're laughing and joking as if they hadn't a care. In about an hour we ought to make a start. The tanks have already commenced to move up; from miles back one can hear the rumble of their progress.

Where shall we be tomorrow? What new march shall we have undertaken? Shall we have broken the line and have sailed off into the blue, pursuing the Hun? Or shall we have finished our last march and be lying very quietly? So long as we break the enemy's line, what happens to anyone of us does not matter. To lie very quietly would be pleasant; we shall have earned a long, unbroken rest.

CHAPTER 18

Protected by the Mist

It's two days since I made my last jotting. How much has happened since then! Since then we've smashed the Hun Front, crumpled it up and swept it back for a distance of fourteen miles. It's difficult to say whether there is any Hun Front left; there's a mob withdrawing in tumultuous retreat and picked suicide-troops, fighting stubborn rear-guard actions.

Today it is our turn to sit down and hold the line in depth. The troops which were behind us yesterday, have leap-frogged us and passed through us. They're fresh and with their unspoilt strength are battering their way still further forward, herding the enemy into panic-stricken groups, and cutting them off from the main body with their tremendous weight of shells. Pressing on their heels, like policemen dispersing a riot, come the ponderous tanks, making no arrests and impersonally bludgeoning every protest into silence.

How far our chaps have penetrated by now we cannot guess, but their guns sound very faintly across the hazy summer distance. Tomorrow we shall again hook in and gallop into the point of the fighting-wedge, while the troops who are up front today will sit tight and hold. This is war as we have always dreamt of it and never hoped to find it.

At last we have our desire: we have leapt out of our trenches, left the filth of No Man's Land behind, and have slipped off into the blue, where we follow a moving battle across plains and wheat-fields to the unravished lands of Germany.

It's the afternoon of August the ninth. It was on the evening of the seventh that we crept out on foot from the shadow of the Boves Woods. The roads were packed with infantry and tanks moving forward in a solid mass; this night everything was moving in the one direction—there was no returning traffic. Hidden in the ravines, just back of the guns, we came across the cavalry, ready to advance the moment a breach in the line had been announced. In contrast with the nervous irritation of other nights, this night there was an uncomplaining austerity. Suspense was nearly at an end, anticipation of dying was soon to be replaced by death's actual presence. The great question in all our minds was, did the Hun know? Had he known all the time? Was he planning to catch us and to forestall our attack by an offensive of his own before morning?

On our arrival at the gun-position in front of the orchard we found that everything was normal and quiet. The odd shell was coming over and bursting with its accustomed regularity in the accustomed places. The enemy had not changed his targets. From his front-line in the valley below us, the normal amount of flares were going up. The machine-gun fire came in irregular bursts and lazily, as if the entire business were a matter of form and not to be taken too much to heart by anybody.

The only noticeable difference was of our making. To drown the throb of our advancing tanks, a great number of bombing-planes had been sent up, which kept flying to and fro at a low altitude above the enemy's trenches. This peaceful state of affairs was too good to last, so we at once set to work feverishly upon our final preparations. Not a man slacked or spared himself; each one knew that before morning his own life might depend upon the honesty of his effort. I don't think, however, it was our own particular lives that concerned us so much as the lives of our pals.

We divided the men into parties, so many to dig the six gun-platforms and so many to sort and stack the ammunition. Every hour or so we changed them over, so that they might not get stale at their task. As soon as the platforms were sufficiently advanced, we man-handled the guns into position and gave them their lines. After that we felt more secure; if the enemy were to anticipate our offensive, we would now be able to reply.

Time did not permit of our constructing sufficient protection for our men; besides, in so exposed a position, we should either escape by reason of the enemy's panic or else get wiped out. We threw up a wall of sandbags and turf about the guns to save their crews from splinters, and dug a more or less splinter-proof hole in which the signallers and the major could do their work. In this hole, by the light of a solitary candle we made out the barrage-table with the times, lifts, rates of fire and ammunition expenditure for the attack, and explained it to the sergeants in charge of the gun-detachments. At 3 a. m. we served the men with hot tea, bully beef and slices of bread. Then we sat down to await developments. Our attack was planned to open at 4.20, just as the dawn would be peeping above the horizon.

Luckily for us a heavy mist had risen up which, as night drew towards morning, had thickened to the density of a fog. It had the effect of blanketing sound. It needed to, for as the tanks lumbered nearer to the front-line to their jumping-off points, the whole world seemed to shake with their clamour. It was like a city of giants marching nearer and forever nearer. Not even the droning of the bombing-planes could drown the ominous breathing of their engines and the clangour of their iron tread.

Whether it was the number and the low altitude of the planes or that the Hun had actually heard the unusual commotion behind our lines, by 3 a. m. he became suspicious. His harassing fire, which usually dies down about that hour, leapt up into a novel intensity. He began to search and sweep new areas, which before had been free from shell-fire, It was a good thing that our work was completed, for we had to throw ourselves down and hug the ground to avoid the splinters. Most of his shells went plus of us and plunged into the orchard behind.

Little sudden illuminations sprang up where piles of ammunition had been struck and were burning. He was evidently making guesses and consulting his map for anything that seemed likely, for when his shelling was working most destruction, he would switch to a new target, where it was wasted. The fog and the night combined, entirely prevented him from seeing what he was doing and from observing the tell-tale conflagrations he had created. We thanked our lucky stars that our position was a bad one and that we weren't in the orchard.

The most nerve-racking moments in any fight are the moments preceding the start of the fight. One suddenly becomes possessed of extraordinary lucidity, somewhat similar to the clarity of thought which is said to be experienced by the drowning. He reviews his entire life in a flash, its failures, successes, unkindnesses and follies. He appreciates with ineffectual poignancy the affections he has wasted and the generosities he has omitted. It is as though, after having walked through all his years, he unexpectedly went aeroplaning and saw below him the panorama of his chances and achievements; he sees the might-have-been high-roads he could have taken, leading to white cities on the hills, and the crooked lanes he did actually choose, losing themselves in quagmire.

Most particularly, in the moments of waiting, he thinks of children, because they are immortality. He wishes with a passionate regret that he had foreseen this hour, and could have left someone behind him who would perpetuate his body long after it has been obliterated and defiled. All the purposes and dignities for which he was created become miraculously obvious to him now. He feels a dull resentment that this clearness of vision was denied him till the power to choose was beyond his choice.

Sometimes this startling mental lucidity takes the form of an unnatural clairvoyance; he acutely apprehends happenings which are out of all possible reach of his senses. His imagination becomes abnormally alert. Lying beneath the weight of darkness, hanging over the lip of the valley, divided from the enemy by a sea of fog, I saw with absolute distinctness the frenzy which was in progress behind the hostile lines. I retain pictures which are as clean-cut as if they had been witnessed. Nine-tenths of the opposing army are sleeping. The sentries have been posted, the distress signals have been arranged and the batteries allotted their several tasks. At sunset everything seems serene; but as night settles down and the mist rises, an unaccountable uneasiness oppresses the spirits of the one-tenth who watch.

Each man feels it, but he fears to voice his alarm till he has proofs which would warrant it. He notes the unusual number of planes in the air; but they are neither machine-gunning nor bombing, and on account of the intense darkness they cannot spy. He may report their presence to headquarters, but there are no grounds for being disturbed so long as they are doing no harm. Besides, he is no expert; he may be mistaken as to their numbers. Then, little by little, above their drone he hears another sound—the sound as of a tidal wave travelling towards him, growing more menacing and taller as it approaches. He peers into the fog and imagines stealthy figures moving. The scurrying of a rat makes him break into a cold sweat. He calls to the next sentry; but his voice will not carry. He realizes that whatever happens, he is alone and cut off. His flares and rockets, if he fires them, will bring him no assistance; they will be smothered by the mountainous wall of whiteness. Fear seizes him, which he can no longer master; at the same time the same fear seizes every other watcher. By telephone or runner they each one send back tidings of their terror.

But the nine-tenths of the enemy who are sleeping are annoyed at being disturbed. "It is nothing," they declare. The news spreads slowly from battalion to brigade, brigade to division, division to corps, from corps to army. Each headquarters, peevish at being aroused and hesitant about arousing its next senior headquarters, wastes time in checking back to the watcher in the front-line for confirmation of his doubts. What is it that he fears? No attack is to be expected; the Allies' storm-troops are up north. There is positive evidence of that fact. The worst that can be looked for is a local raiding-party. What are the reasons for his panic?

The reasons for his panic! They are vague, indefinite; he has no reasons—only intuitions, doubts, conjectures. He knows that the night is black and that he is filled with a horrible foreboding.

There are too many men over there across No Man's Land. He cannot prove it, but he can feel their bated breath.

Reluctantly the nine-tenths of the army who were sleeping, are awakened. They lie listening in their deep dugouts, unwilling to believe that calamity threatens. Then suddenly, when it is too late to be prepared, the suspicion strengthens that a major offensive will open with the morning. There is only an hour till dawn—too little time to act. The infantry are ordered to stand to in the trenches and the batteries to increase their rate of fire. Messages are sent to the rear to hurry up the reserves. Brigades of artillery, which are out at rest, hook in and start forward at the gallop. Even the most autocratic old generals are convinced and, to save their reputations, forsake their beds and become officiously important. Meanwhile, the men in the front-line shiver in the darkness. They know that they have no chance now and are merely waiting to be slaughtered.

And we, on our side of No Man's Land, we wait also. We do not like the job in hand; we were not born to be butchers. We are very much the same as those chaps over there. If we could, we would prefer to live our lives out, shake hands with the enemy and go home to our families. We have no quarrel with them individually; but we have no means of telling them that. It seems stupid to have come so far, to have suffered such hardships, to have sat up so many weary nights, simply in order to do something for which four years ago we should have been hanged. But we can't wriggle out of it. If we tried to break away, all along the roads of France armed men are stationed to turn us back.

We are impotent to express any choice in the matter. Certain people have quarrelled—people who do not wear khaki and who will never face death at sunrise. Who they are and why they should have quarrelled, we do not properly understand. Probably they muddled themselves into this row; how they did it, they themselves could not tell us. They're kings and statesmen and nobs—far too high up for us to criticise. All we know is that we are their sacrifice. Because they say it is right, the more men we kill at dawn, the more glory we shall earn. Later on, if we survive the war and kill only one man, they will tell us it is wrong, and we shall end on the scaffold.

It's all very puzzling—devilishly puzzling, when one's brains and hands and feet are numbed with cold. It's always perishing at three in the morning But these thoughts don't do a chap any good; there's nothing to be gained by philosophising. It's been going on for four years now—this living in mud and bathing in sweat, and always killing something. God hasn't spoken. He must know what he wants.

At 3.45 a. m. the sergeants reported that all their fuses were set. At four o'clock the whistle was blown for the "stand to" and the gun-crews crouched behind their guns in readiness. They needed to crouch, for the enemy shelling was finding us out and growing momentarily in intensity. Evidently more of their artillery was coming up and getting into action. From four o'clock onwards every five minutes the whistle blew and through the darkness a spectral voice announced: "Fifteen minutes to go"; "ten minutes to go"; "five minutes to go." From far and wide behind the fog other whistles were heard sounding, and other voices making the same announcement.

The last five minutes were counted off separately and the final minute in intervals of ten seconds: "Thirty seconds to go, twenty, ten, five." Then, "Let her rip," and a shrill blast of the whistle.

As though red-hot needles were stabbing at the drums, our ears are ringing and deafened. The air quivers and the ground files up as if it were about to open. Our eyes are scorched by a marching wall of flame, against which are etched our rapid gunners, hurling hell across the valley like men demented, and our gallant eighteen-pounders barking, recoiling and bristling like infuriated terriers. We're off with a vengeance. The greatest offensive of the war has started. Shall we get away with it in so advanced a position? At all events, it's an end of waiting—that at least is a comfort.

CHAPTER 19

All Systems Go

Yesterday's attack was a complete success—so complete that, in spite of all our preparations, its magnitude took us unaware. Had anyone had the faith to foresee a Hun defeat of such dimensions, we should have been able to have made a more deadly use of our advantage. As it was we lost a certain amount of time and, as a consequence, wasted some of our chances.

The trouble was, as usual, that we were controlled too much from the rear by staff-people, who didn't come upfront to see what was happening for themselves, but gathered all their information second and third-hand. When the psychological moment had arrived for us to go forward, they became nervous and held us back. There were interminable telephone conversations with observers, liaison-officers, battery-commanders, all and sundry, before they could be persuaded that we were not proposing to put our heads into a trap.

Staff-people are the most incorrigible pessimists. They will never believe the fighter when he sends back word that victory is in his hands. They make him leave off fighting to answer foolish questions; by the time they permit him to go on fighting the enemy has very frequently recovered himself. They are so cursed with a fatal belief in their own omniscience that they scarcely credit the combatants, who run all the risks, with sense.

In the old days battles were won by generals who led their troops in person, sharing the dangers and setting an example by their courage. They were on the spot as eye-witnesses, and recognized to a second when the moment to take hazards had arrived. Today of necessity our generals and their staffs are desk-men, with the natural caution and scepticism of deskmen. They sit far back of the line, remote from shell-fire, in *chateaux* fitted out like surveyors' offices with typewriters, photographs, scales and maps.

They do all their fighting on paper. When they are directing an attack, they collect their information by telephone, doubt it, sift it, weigh it, ponder it and discuss it, when lightning action is all that is required. Many of them have never been anything but deskmen since this war started; their combatant experience was gained years ago in little sporting rough-and-tumbles with aborigines on the outskirts of civilization. Because they have never personally endured the modern hell into which they have to fling their men, they can form no mental picture of the situations that occur, and the prompt action that should be taken. They are equipped for planning the preliminary details of a show; but their control of an attack, when once it has started, is paralysing. So much is this the case that it's a common saying among the men that the battles which we win in the trenches are lost by the staff-people who are behind.

On the morning of August the eighth the weather conditions were all in our favour. The fog was worth several extra divisions to us. It kept the enemy guessing. We knew what we intended to do, but he had to find out. The fog enabled us to conceal our intentions up to the very last moment. Until we were upon him, he had no knowledge of the directions from which we were approaching; by the time we were upon him it was too late for him to take the proper defensive steps. The first warning he had was when out of the deathly stillness our murderous barrage came roaring and screaming about his head.

Never on any front has there been so tremendous a concentration of guns as we let loose on him that morning. The weight of shells and mass of explosives that we threw over him literally rolled up the landscape and pinned everything living to the ground. It passed over his trench-system like a gigantic plough, burying men and weapons, and travelled on into the distance by a pre-arranged series of leaps and bounds. The tanks, following the curtain of fire and lumbering ahead of the infantry, trampled into flatness whatever resistance the creeping barrage had spared.

While the heavens were raining brimstone and fire up front, his back-country was faring no better, for every battery position, strong-point, support-trench, cross-road, regimental headquarters and camp of which we had knowledge was kept under continual bombardment by our siege-guns and heavies. Meanwhile our cavalry of the air were flying low along his roads, by which retreat was possible, machine-gunning and bombing. It was like stopping up all the holes and smoking a wild beast out of his lair.

The remnants of his front-line garrison, who had not been pulverised by our tanks or buried by our shelling, threw away their arms and came streaming through the dawn to encounter the mercy of our bayonets. Later, those who had been taken prisoners, straggled in groups of twos and threes past our guns. They looked more like animals than men, their eyes glaring, their heads nodding, their steps tottering. Some of them walked shufflingly, like blinded men, groping for their direction. Others ran panting at a wolf-trot, as if they still felt that they were pursued by death. All of them were polluted with the unspeakable stench of carnage; behind the smoke of battle, before we saw them, we could smell them coming.

If the weather conditions favoured our infantry and tanks, they were even more favourable to ourselves. Had there been no fog, the moment we opened fire our flashes would have been spotted, our positions on the map discovered and our batteries wiped out. As it was our flashes, as seen through the fog from the enemy's commanding height of land, must have appeared a composite blur of flame, flickering across the landscape for miles from right to left. He made a strenuous effort to bombard us, but was hopelessly inaccurate and out for range. After shelling us in a random fashion for perhaps fifteen minutes, he seemed to get wind of the disaster that had happened up front and, putting his guns out of action, drew them back. When he opened up again, his shells came slowly, as though from a great distance, and landed anywhere and everywhere, haphazard.

The dawn rose slowly, as though reluctant to look upon our handiwork. If it seemed slow to us, how much slower it must have seemed to the men whom we were slaughtering. There was no rush of golden splendour, no valiant peering of the sun above a treed horizon—only a thinly diffused pallor, shapeless and ghastly, which made the mist appear more impenetrable than ever. Day evaded us, hiding his chalky face in his hands, like a clown who had gazed on tragedy. When light came there was no laughter in its glance; it was a dead thing drifting in a stagnant emptiness.

The flashes of the guns tore rents in the filmy obscurity by which we were surrounded, but they could not disperse it. Our eyes were smarting, our ears deafened, our senses astounded. The ground beneath our feet quivered as though it were the crust of a volcano. Our nerves shied at each fresh concussion, and our bodies trembled. We longed for the sky to become clear that we might learn what was happening. We had signalling parties attached to the infantry with flags and lamps. It had been arranged beforehand that we should watch various points in the captured country for their messages. If they had tried to send any back, none had been observed.

As the strafe progressed, the mist was made doubly dense by the reek of battle. The atmosphere became choking with the fumes of high explosives and the enemy, in a desperate effort to silence us, commenced to shell us with gas. We lit innumerable cigarettes to steady our nerves and carried on mechanically with our destructive work. Running from gun-platform to gun-platform, we checked up the lays of the gunners. Every few minutes the whistle sounded for a lift in the barrage, and there was a momentary pause in the crash of discharge while the angle was changed and the range lengthened.

Along the road to our left, where shells were falling, ambulances lurched and panted, leaving behind a trail of blood. Wounded Tommies staggered by, with their arms about the shoulders of wounded Huns. Meeting these derelicts who were returning, fresh companies of supporting infantry moved up, undaunted by the spectacle of a fate which they might share. At the sight of us firing they waved their caps shouting, "That's the stuff to give 'em. Give 'em one for us, boys. Give 'em hell."

At what hour it happened I cannot say for certain; the mist was clearing, the sun was beginning to be merry and the air was streaky with lavender-tinted smoke, when between the pollarded trees of the high-road batteries of French seventy-fives appeared, gallantly trotting to the carnage. They were the first of the sacrifice batteries moving up. Shells burst to right and to left of them; one fell directly among them. It made no difference; the guns and wagons which were behind, swerving aside and round the struggling mass, passed determinedly on to meet the vaster horror which lay before them. The drivers, sitting stiffly erect as on parade, rose and fell to the movement of the horses. The gunners clung tightly to the jolting vehicles, no tremor of emotion showing on their faces. They were going into open warfare, where men die cleanly among wheatfields. The sight was superb and filled us with envy.

We had been firing at extreme range for some time; now at last across the wire the order came to stand down. This meant that where our shells had been falling, our infantry were preparing to advance; it also meant that unless we hooked in and followed up, we should be permanently out of action.

We felt disgraced to sit there doing nothing, while crowds of those about to die streamed past us. Yes, streamed past us; they came in droves, these young lads with their keen, bronzed faces. They came singing and twirling their caps on their bayonets, as if fear were an emotion unknown to their hearts. They came brushing through the wheat, following the tracks the tanks had made; they came cheering up the ravines and laughing along the highroad. They came carrying rifles, machine-guns, trench-mortars, bombs—all the filthy inventions war has brought to perfection, whereby one man may torture another. They stuck wildflowers in their tunics, as if off on a holiday. They never once acknowledged by word or gesture that life might hold for them no more tomorrows. Brave hearts! And always as they passed, seeing us sitting beside our silent guns with our still more silent faces, they would throw back gay taunts about meeting us in Germany.

We could not taunt back; we felt ourselves a farce. In our minds we saw the French sacrifice batteries going at the gallop into action, "Halt, action front," popping off their rounds, hooking in again, and going on and on forever. Why had we been forced to march so far if, now that we were here, they did not intend to use us? They'd shown precious little consideration up to now; and now, when the battle was raging and we were needed and ought not to be spared, they were willing to spare us. Death didn't in the least matter, if only we could earn our share in the glory.

Our little major was fuming, mutinous and twitching with impatience, when Heming rode up and saluted, bringing the news that he had the teams, wagons and limbers halted behind the orchard. In a trice the major was on the 'phone, pleading for permission to breeze off with us into the blue and take a chance. His request was curtly refused; our division of artillery was to stay where it was and to hold the line in depth, in case the infantry was driven back by the Huns.

Major Charlie Wraith kicked the 'phone over in his anger. He said a good many things which could quite easily have earned him a court-martial. Hold the line in depth, indeed—an old woman's precaution! This was a fine time to be playing safe, when our infantry were out there, forging miles ahead without guns to protect them. If they got beaten back, whose fault would that be with no artillery to support them? It was the old story of the staff-people losing the battle for us. If victory were turned into defeat, the way it was at Cambrai, we should have our red-tabs to thank for it. It was about half-an-hour after this disappointment that belated word came through that the enemy's resistance was stiffening and an attack was pending. One section from each battery had to go forward under two junior officers. Ours was ordered to report to the 11th Battalion and to act under the direction of the infantry colonel. Its job was to follow within sight of the attack and to come into action in the open, if necessary, for the purpose of knocking out machine-gun nests or any other obstacles which were holding up the advance.

The major turned to me. "You will take your section, and Tubby Grain will go with you."

As he walked away his throat thickened with something very like a sob. "By God, I'd revert to a one-pip artist and I'd give the very shirt off my back to see what you lads are going to see this morning,"

CHAPTER 20

Title

We started off at 9 a. m. feeling like a pair of generals, Tubby and I with our brace of eighteen-pounders, our ammunition-wagons and our men. We were setting out practically as free-lances, to discover our own chances of glory. The only senior officer to whom we had to report was the battalion-colonel; there was no one in the rear with whom we had to keep in touch, who would have the power to hold us back. How much fighting we would see before dusk fell depended entirely upon our own initiative. We intended to see a lot.

We had been given maps, which would carry us about fif-teen miles into what had been the enemy's country. We had been given rations to last one meal for the men and horses, the usual twenty-four hours' allowance for the battery not having arrived when we made our start. The major promised to follow us up with provisions later, if that were possible; if it were not, we would have to forage for ourselves. In view of the extremely meagre break-fast we had had, this shortness of supplies was the one small cloud on our otherwise bright horizon. The last sight we had as we pulled out on our journey was the tragically covetous faces of the companions from whom we were parting. "Goodbye, old things," they shouted. "Win a V. C. apiece. If you don't, you're not worth your salt."

The road down to Domart was by this time heavily crowded with transport moving in both directions. The traffic moving forward consisted for the most part of tanks and lorries, carrying up infantry and ammunition. The returning traffic was made up almost solely of prisoners, walking wounded and motor-transport bringing back our casualties. At first it was necessary to proceed at the walk in a crawling procession, which often halted. As Tubby rode beside me at the head of our column, we planned our individual campaign together. We arranged that I would lead the guns, while he rode ahead with mounted signallers and sent me back my targets. We weren't going to miss a trick; we were going to take everything. Wherever there was a machine-gun to be knocked out, we'd be there to do it.

Through the stench and reek of battle the sun was shining valiantly. With the melting of the fog, our sense of tension had vanished. We felt tremendously sporting, as though we were riding out to a day of hunting. To keep our thoughts from growing serious, we made up poker hands out of the army numbers on the ambulances that we passed.

Presently Tubby said, "Did you ever think that the thing might happen to you that has happened to those chaps?"

I followed his glance and saw that he was looking at three of our infantry sprawled out by the roadside; they had evidently all three been caught by the one shell. I nodded. "Oh yes, I've thought of that. I expect we all have."

"But I don't mean simply thinking of it," he insisted. "What I mean is have you ever known in your bones that you weren't going to last—that you were going to look exactly as those chaps look before the war is ended?"

"None of us knows that," I said shortly, "and to believe that you know it is morbid."

The worst thing that can happen to a man at the front is for him to get the premonition that he is going to be killed. Whether it is that this feeling really is a warning or that the imagining that he has been forewarned attracts the thing that kills him, it is impossible to tell; it is, however, a fact that the belief seems to destroy a man's magic immunity and one usually hears of his death within a short time of his making such a confession.

"I'm not morbid." Tubby spoke quite wholesomely. "I'm not

going queer, the way some chaps do, and I'm not afraid. I'm not asking you to be sorry for me, and I'm not pitying myself. If I were given the choice I'd sooner go west out here, doing something average decent, than drag on into peace times and disappoint myself. And I should disappoint myself; you know that."

"Don't worry yourself, old son," I replied cheerfully; "you're not the only one. We shall all disappoint ourselves."

He nodded. "Yes, every man disappoints himself, but not all along the line, the way I should, because of one wrong act. I was only a kid when I crossed from Canada and I was horribly lonely and I don't suppose this is in the least interesting to you; I'll put it briefly and then we'll talk of something else. There was a girl and she seemed kind—not at all the sort of girl with whom I could be happy. I didn't marry her and since I've been out here . . ."

He didn't finish his sentence.

"She's been blackmailing you?" I asked. "A lot of that's done."

He stared me honestly between the eyes. "Worse than that. It's been hell. She writes me there's another coming."

Without giving me a chance to reply, he whirled his horse about and went away at a trot to the rear of the column.

Poor little Tubby! What a lot it must have cost him to be always cheerful and smiling. I understood now why he had gambled so heavily and, however much he won, had always remained in debt. What a nightmare his experience of war must have been to him, continually facing up to death with the knowledge that every time he came back alive the bill for the old sin would once more be presented. His case can be multiplied by thousands.

From the start of the war there have been girls who have made a trade of preying on the consciences of men who are risking their all in the trenches. Half the time their trump-card, that there is a child, is no more than a mean lie by means of which to extract money. In the light of this little glimpse of pitiful biography, the world to which we had said goodbye seemed full of treacherous traps to betray our manhood; this thing which we were now doing, despite its terrible cruelty, was clean and straight and redemptive. You rode into action with the sun shining to do one strong thing and, if need be, to die when your courage was at its highest. There wasn't much to regret about that. It was easy to be good when to be brave was all that was required.

We had come down to Domart, the little village on the edge of No Man's Land, from which the offensive had started. The houses were bent and twisted. Their roofs were gone and their walls gaped with ugly holes where shells had torn through them. Of those which still stood, there was scarcely one which had not had a side taken out. Some of them were in flames; others had caved in and sprawled black and smouldering. The ruins were filled with poisonous odours, gas, blood, decay, the fumes of explosives.

Yet one noted the heroism of the little gardens which had somehow contrived to outlive this hell. Trees were dead and stood limply with their arms blown off or hanging laboriously at their sides by a shred; but flowers still smiled and lifted up their faces. All along the streets, outside improvised dressing-stations, our wounded lay on stretchers. There was no moaning—no giving way to pity. However terrible their wounds, they rested there in the sun with the blood drying on their cheeks, perfectly motionless and apparently happy that for a time their fighting days were ended. They were mostly blue and gray-eyed men, simple and childish looking in their helplessness.

The stretcher-bearers were Hun prisoners, depressed fellows, who perspired freely beneath their enormous steel helmets and the bulky haversacks which they carried on their shoulders. They plodded to and fro like dumb animals, docile, obedient and eager to ingratiate themselves. One wondered why at dawn we should have attempted to kill each other, when a few hours later we could get along so comfortably.

On the far side of the village we began to climb the heavily entrenched slope, which the enemy had held that morning. Nothing of his trench-system was left. The shell-holes were nearly all fresh and stretched lip to lip as far as Dodo Wood, proving the accuracy and intensity of our barrage. However many men had perished, hardly a trace of them was left; they had been buried by the unseen thing that had murdered them.

At the edge of Dodo Wood a mounted man met us, bringing a message that the battalion we were supporting would probably attack at noon, and appointing as our place of rendezvous a deep ravine several miles ahead. We had lost so much time through halts in the traffic that it was already very nearly eleven. If we were to keep our appointment, our only chance was to strike off to the left across country and risk being still further delayed by wire entanglements and shell-holes. We picked up the track of one of our tanks and followed it round the edge of a high plateau.

It was curious to note how very slightly the plateau was fortified. The enemy must have been hugely confident of his ability to hold that ground. Here and there he had established strongpoints, which our tanks had discovered and stamped flat; but of trenches there were hardly any. One saw extraordinarily few dead and none at all of our own fellows. It was obvious that the enemy had not tried to make a stand; the moment his front-line had been overwhelmed all the forces which were behind him had broken and fled, allowing our chaps to romp home. It was as unlike a modern battle field as you could well imagine. The sun shone and larks sang overhead. Through the trampled wheat every now and then a hare scampered; save ourselves nothing human was in sight, living or dead. The armies of pursuers and pursued had slogged their way forward and vanished into the blue distance that lay ahead.

We came down by a gradual decline to the ravine which had been named as our rendezvous. It was an angry looking place, with steep grassy slopes rising up precipitously on either side and no possible means of escape, when once it had been entered, except by the exits at either end. The ravine, like the plateau, was empty and silent—nothing spoke, nothing stirred. Unlike the plateau it was not merry with wind and sunshine; it was sinister, shadowy, and held a hint of menace. No one was there to meet us; so while Tubby rode on to find the infantry headquarters, I left the section to rest, while I reconnoitred a village about a quarter of a mile distant for a place at which to water the horses. One had to go cautiously in investigating country so recently captured, as there were quite likely to be pockets of Huns left behind, who had been over-looked in the rapidity of the advance. There was also this additional reason for caution, that in a moving battle it was impossible to tell where our front-line was at any particular moment. It would be quite easy to go too far and find oneself in the hands of the enemy.

When I entered the village I found that it was as dead as Sodom. It stank like an open sewer. Into its streets mattresses, broken furniture, every kind of refuse, had been cast. It had evidently only recently been vacated by the enemy, for the signs of his going were everywhere. He must have surrendered it without firing a shot, for the only dead were his own soldiers, who had been killed by our bombardment, and one civilian woman with a little fair-haired child in her arms.

I tied up my horse and with my groom entered several of the houses, thinking that we might find food to help us eke out our rations. The Hun, with a methodical orderliness which almost called for admiration, had anticipated our necessity and, even in the panic of his departure, had not left so much as a loaf of bread. Whatever he could not carry off he had polluted and rendered useless. The only food we found was in a quartermaster's store, where the quartermaster, a man of immense proportions, sat huddled in a chair with a huge skull-wound in his forehead, contemplating a meal which he would never finish, over which the flies hummed a requiem.

We examined the wells behind the houses; all except three of them had been filled with rubbish. We rode down to the river; here the stench we had noticed on entering grew nauseating. Everything that could render the water undrinkable had been flung into it; dead men, dead horses and indescribable offal. It was horrible, this irreverent use they had made of men who had been their comrades. While we watched the little river which yesterday had been so clean and happy, strangling between its grassy banks, we heard the jingling of swords and the sharp trit-trotting of horsemen approaching.

Round a bend in the empty street came the first of our cavalry, their chargers side-stepping and prancing, and their men bending forward with an expression of smiling expectancy. They were the most gallant sight of a gallant morning, these magnificent animals, dumb and human, who had waited throughout the war for their chance and now, like unleashed hounds, came running hot upon the scent, eager to prove their mettle. The sight of them was inspiring and instinct with intelligence; it lifted the mere toil of killing out of its monotony and into the rarer atmosphere of valour.

They drew up by the river, but only for a moment. The dainty creatures lowered their muzzles to the water, screamed and jumped back, shaking their heads. They looked like high-born ladies, fresh from the toilet, scented and washed and contemptuous of anything that would soil their perfection. There was a look of inexhaustible youth about them, as though they had been pampered with the promise of unescapable immortality.

With a hunting cry and a touch of the spur, they went bounding off through the shining weather, leaving behind a memory which set a standard.

We were to see them not so many hours later, when their glory had been accomplished.

CHAPTER 21

Carnage

We watered our horses out of the buckets at the few wells which had not been poisoned. It was a lengthy process, but we were all finished and ready to move off by the time Tubby returned. He brought word that it had been found impossible to pull off the attack at the hour set. The country in front of us was studded with woods and cut up by gorges, which the enemy was holding with machine-guns. Moreover, by retiring the Hun had shortened the distance for his supports to come up and was now numerically much stronger than had at first been imagined. The bulk of our artillery were too far back to be brought up, so the tasks which ought to have been undertaken by the guns were to be carried out by bombing-planes. As soon as these were ready the assault would commence. Meanwhile our instructions were to push on to the head of the ravine and remain there concealed till we were ordered forward.

"It's going to be a pretty sporting show, if I know anything about it," Tubby said, when we were once again on the march. "The infantry are fed up to the back-teeth with the way in which the guns have failed to keep in touch with them. And I don't wonder—you wait till you see the kind of country they've got to tackle. It's no joke being a lone man on two legs, with hundreds of field-guns pointing at you and quite as many machine-guns singing your swan-song in the woods, and all their stuff coming over and none of yours going back. It's a bit stiff to tell chaps to advance against that, as though you expected 'em to strangle whole batteries with their naked hands. It's up to us to show them that the eighteen-pounders aren't quitters. We'll take as long a chance as any of them. If some of us aren't pushing daisies by sunset, it won't be our fault."

Out of the corner of my eye I watched him. He wasn't the same man who had made that shabby little confession to me earlier in the morning. He had been weak and conscience-haunted then; now he was eager and heroic. One no longer noticed that he was fat and good-natured and ordinary; a new boldness and dignity transformed him. The test of scarlet was discovering chivalrous values in Tubby of which he himself was only partly aware.

As though he recognised my thoughts, he nodded, "I'm happy. I wouldn't have missed today for worlds."

To the south of us, like hail-stones pounding on a roof of metal, a heavy bombardment had been steadily growing in violence. It was the French putting on an attack. Probably the seventy-fives we had seen trotting into action that morning were in it. Good luck to them. As suddenly as it had opened, it died down, and was succeeded by the crackling of rifle-fire. We pictured the blue-clad tiger-men of France going over, dropping on one knee to take aim, then up and on again to slake the thirst of their bayonets.

With a kind of glee, Tubby whispered, " Our turn next."

Up to this point the ravine had been bare of any signs of battle; now dramatically, as we rounded a spur in the hillside, we found ourselves gazing on a scene which made us catch our breath. This must have been one of the enemy's camps, cleverly selected because of the shelter which the steeply sloping banks afforded. The open space between the banks was so narrow that it looked like an emptied riverbed.

In this open space were wagons, arrested in the act of pulling out. The drivers still sat on their seats, as though overcome by sleep, with their heads sagging against their breasts and the reins held limply in their hands. The teams still hooked to the vehicles, had crumpled forward in the traces. The doors of all the little wooden shacks along the side of the ravine were wide open. Between them and the wagons men lay sprawled upon the turf, as though caught midway in the act of running. The only living things which stirred, were wounded horses of appalling leanness, which were feebly grazing and on seeing us, tottered a few steps, and then waited, as if asking us to come to their help.

Instinctively, without an order being given, the entire column behind us halted. Death is horrible enough when it looks like death; but when it mimics life, it applauds its own terror. At first we had the feeling that we had stumbled on a sleepy hollow; were we to make a noise, all these sleeping forms would waken and rise from the ground.

How had the tragedy happened? Had our guns, after having allowed them to believe themselves secure, deluged them with shells when the dawn was breaking? Or had our bombing-planes discovered them at the moment when they were escaping? However they had died, it was easy to reconstruct the scene's mercilessness and agony. In contemplating it, we felt a momentary shame. The cowardice of war is forever treading hard on the heels of its valour. These men had had no chance to defend themselves. They had not seen the men by whom they were murdered. They had been roused from sleep by a commotion, to find death raining on them from the air.

As we renewed our advance, we discovered that not all of the men were dead. Some looked up with dimming eyes as we passed. They neither approved nor condemned us. They were beyond all that. We had neither the time nor the materials to help them. The shell-dressing, which we each carried, we might need for ourselves before the day was out. We had not dared to fill our water-bottles at the wells in the village; so our supplies were only what we had brought with us, and they were fast getting exhausted.

When we came to the head of the ravine, we were glad that we had not given water to the enemy, for there we found our own wounded scattered through the grass. They were too far forward for the stretcher-bearers to reach them for many hours yet. There was no one with the means or time to spend upon them; we were all fighting-men, under orders to press on at any moment. Nevertheless our gunners slipped down from the limbers and went among them, pouring the last of their water between their parching lips. At the sight of their suffering an illogical anger seized us against the brutes who had done this to men who were ours.

We did not reason that we also were trying to wound and kill; we only felt a blazing indignation that those boys, who had passed through our guns cheering so gallantly in the early morning, should lie so silent now. After this, when an enemy asked for water, we turned from him in contempt; whatever drops we had to spare were for our friends. Mounted and eager to go forward, we sat pitilessly among the dying enemy.

We were there not to show mercy, but to avenge.

The sun grew dark while we waited; then rapidly the rain descended. We caught it in our cupped hands and on our tongues as it dripped from the edge of our steel helmets. The wounded in the grass lay back with their blackened lips wide apart, sucking in the moisture which the heavens, indifferently impartial, allowed to fall on both enemies and friends.

Tubby and his signallers had again gone forward to make connections with the infantry. I had arranged with him that we would follow in close support the moment he sent back word that the advance had commenced. By the number of planes that were in the air we knew that the moment was at hand.

I glanced back at my men, trying to estimate how they had been affected by the scenes which they had already witnessed. In trench-warfare the gunners and drivers rarely see a battlefield until long after the wounded have been collected and carried back. They never see their own infantry in the act of attacking, and they never see the bursting of their own shells. In a few minutes all these new experiences were to be theirs. There were no signs of trepidation on their faces—only an expression of stern and happy elation.—On the top of the bank one of Tubby's mounted signallers appeared, waving his flag. I gave the order to "Walk, March," then to trot, and we were off.

For the first half mile we could see nothing very unusual. In front of us and on every side, climbing a gentle slope to the sky-line, was a vast wheatfield scarcely trampled. Here and there we saw a fallen man, who seemed only to be taking his rest. As far as evidences of battle were concerned, we might have been out on manoeuvres. As we neared the sky-line, I halted the guns and rode forward with my signallers. Over the crest a very different sight presented itself. The wheatfield ended and a splendid stretch of country, green and cool, resembling a parkland, commenced. Floating like islands in the greenness were dense clumps of trees.

On the farthest edge of the plain were deep ravines, a ridge and barriers of woods, above which were church spires and the roofs of houses. The atmosphere, washed clean by rain and made golden by the afternoon sunshine, was so clear that one's eyesight carried for miles and picked out each isolated movement. In the foreground our infantry wandered in apparently leisurely fashion, going forward in little groups of from five to ten. Every now and then a shell would burst near them or the turf would fly up in spurts of dust where a machine-gun had been brought to bear on them. Then they would scatter, throwing themselves flat. Presently some of them would rise and wander on again; those who did not rise would roll over once or twice, as a man does when he settles himself in bed, and then, having found his comfort, lies motionless. The thing was so quickly done that, for the beholder, it was robbed of its terror.

In front of the infantry the cavalry were in action. They pricked in and out the clumps of trees, not galloping or even trotting, but unhurriedly, as if out for an afternoon's pleasure. The sun shone on their drawn blades and, over the green distance, at intervals their trumpets sounded.

Ahead of the cavalry the tanks nosed round the edges of the woods, dragging their bellies along the ground like satiated dragons. Now and then they spat fire and were lost to sight in undergrowth and deep shadows; usually when they re-appeared, there were little dots of smoke-gray pigmies fleeing calamitously before them. Along the ridge on the far horizon a road ran, which was black with escaping ants. Out of the ravines and gorges, leading up to the road, more panic-stricken ants swarmed tumultuously. Above them, darting and swooping like swallows after gnats, flew our bombing-planes and scouts. It was all very sylvan and picturesque—more like a pageant which had been rehearsed and staged than the most dramatic happening in a war which had excelled all other wars in drama.

Half a mile away a flag began to wave; I read the signal and turned back to lead my guns into action. As we came out of the wheatfield at the gallop a general tried to stop us, shouting questions as to where we were going. We simply pointed ahead and went by him without slackening our pace. We downed trail behind a hedge and commenced firing over open sights; our target was the enemy transport retreating along the ridge. As our shrapnel began to burst in little puffs of smoke above the heads of an enemy already mad with terror, the wildest confusion resulted. Lorries were ditched. Batteries became entangled. Horses stampeded through the crowds of flying men, knocking them down and grinding their bodies beneath the wheels of the vehicles.

The enthusiasm of our gunners rose to fever-pitch when for the first time they could see the havoc which their shells were working. They became careless of their own safety and indifferent to death, if only we could push the Boche further back and make the day completely victorious. The same self-forgetfulness was seen on every hand. Out there in that green picture-world, the cavalry were pushing impetuously far ahead. They were so impatient to get forward that, when they were held up by machine-gun nests, they would not wait for the other arms to come up, but were charging the storm of lead with their naked steel and riding to almost certain annihilation.

V. C.s were being won under our eyes by men whose heroism would not even be recorded. And no one cared—no one coveted glory for himself. We were fanatics, lifted far above self-seeking. It was the game that counted. Dust we were and to dust we would return; but the triumph of this day would live forever.

Distracting us from the white intensity of our effort we heard the droning of an engine and saw a shadow settling down; above our heads an aeroplane was hovering so low that we could see the moving lips of the pilot. A message, attached to yellow streamers, came drifting down. When the pilot was sure that we had received it, he again flew off up front. The message gave us the map-location of a machine-gun in action, which we were asked to do our best to knock out. Soon Tubby was again seen frantically signalling. He was telling us that the enemy, while undoubtedly in full retreat, was leaving behind him picked sui-cide-troops to hold machine-gun nests and strong-points. These people were lying doggo till our tanks had gone past them and were then resurrecting themselves and mowing down our men. We limbered up and once more went forward, the signallers and myself going in advance, the guns and ammunition-wagons strung out at safe intervals behind us.

We came across the parkland to a deep cutting, which was the entrance to a gorge. There was nothing to warn one that the cutting was there until the moment before he stood gazing down into it. The hollow between the two banks was full of dead cavalry. Some of the horses were sitting up on their haunches like dogs, swaying their heads slowly from side to side. One by one they would struggle to rise, only to sink back in despair. The riders lay beside their mounts, with their sword-arms flung wide and the sunlight flickering along their blades. From the semi-circle in which they were spread out, one judged that they had made their charge fan-wise, concentrating as they neared the object of their attack. One man out of so many had reached his objective; he had ridden down the Hun machine-gunner, burying the gun beneath the body of his horse and sabring the gunner as he fell.

And these were the magnificent exponents of glory whom I had seen in their pride that morning, prancing through the polluted village so capriciously that their feet seemed to spurn the ground. They had done their bit and by their sacrifice had brought us one step nearer to victory. It was heroic and magnanimous; but, when I remembered the beauty of their vigour as they bounded to the music of their hunting-calls, I could not believe that any gain was worth their anguish. The horrible unfairness of war was all that I could visualize—that one man behind a machine-gun should be able to transmute so much loveliness into corruption in a handful of seconds. And then came another thought—the desire for revenge.

There was the sound of heavy firing further up the gorge. Tubby came riding back; his right arm was hanging loosely and a bullet had seared his forehead. His face was tense.. The little beast he rode was flecked with blood and wildly excited. He broke into a broad grin at catching sight of me. "By the Lord Harry, we've got our chance," he panted. "My arm! No, it's nothing—broken I guess. There's a place up here just behind a bend; if we can sneak a gun in quickly, we can blow the stuffing out of them. We'll be on to them before they know we're there. It's a regular nest, four or five of 'em spurting away like blazes. They've nailed our chaps so that they can't budge. But if we look lively, it's a cinch; we've got them cold."

Following him cautiously, we came to the bend he had mentioned Twenty yards short, we unhooked and ran the gun up by hand. Had we driven straight on to the position, the heads of the horses would have shown up and we should have been wiped out before we had fired our first round. As it was there was a bunch of scrub, just tall enough to hide us. Peering through the branches, we could see about five hundred yards distant a barricade constructed of timbers and sandbags, from which came vicious sprays of death. Repeated endeavours had to be made to rush it. In front and all around lay our fallen infantry, their rifles with fixed bayonets tossed aside and their fingers dug into the turf. The postures in which they had collapsed were violently grotesque. There was forlornness, but little dignity about their twisted attitudes.

Behind the sandbags there was a sense of watching eyes; but only the sense—one saw no movement. The men who kept guard there were brave. They hadn't a chance in the world. They must have known that their fate was sealed from the first. They were selling their lives dearly that their comrades, fleeing behind them, might gain time. Those comrades would never know how they had died—would never be able to thank them. There would be no Iron Crosses to reward their valour—they would be lucky if they were awarded the decency of a grave. We acknowledged their courage, and we hated them.

Our first shot went plus, our second minus, our third scored a direct hit on the barricade. As the sandbags crumbled and the gray uniforms became plain, our infantry leapt from their places of hiding, charging up the gorge with their cold bayonets. We saw hands thrust up in an appeal for mercy, then nothing but khaki, stabbing and cheering wildly. When we had hooked in and rode by five minutes later, four men in smoke-gray lay watching the sky with unblinking eyes. They were decent looking men, with flaxen hair and high complexions. They were perfectly ordinary individuals, with nothing either noticeably noble or brutal in their appearance.

Had we encountered them as waiters in a London or New York restaurant, they would probably have proved entirely in keeping with their situation. By the accident of war they had been called upon to perform a deed quite as desperate as that of the Roman Horatius, who kept the bridge against un-numbered foes. The gorge was one of the keys to the great plain across which the Huns were retiring. These four men, single-handed, with no hope of saving their own lives, had held up our advance for half an hour against repeated infantry and cavalry charges, accounting for fully twenty times their own number in casualties. It was an act of superb sacrifice, which could only have been inspired by the highest sense of duty and patriotism. Had we met them in fable, we should have done them homage; meeting them where we did, we clubbed them like rats escaping from a cage. Even now that they were dead we detested them.

At the top of the gorge we struck a level stretch of country, which appeared to be surrounded by a solid belt of forest; but from the map we learnt that the forest was actually made up of separate woods between which passed channels of sward. Hidden in these separate woods were towns and villages, the spires of whose churches peeped above the trees and speared the horizon. Across the plain ran a network of white roads, some of which were mere tracks trampled out of the chalk by military traffic, others of which dated back to the days before the coming of the Germans. The main road was the one which we had shelled from our first position. It was littered with men, horses, broken limbers, guns and abandoned transport.

A hospital-tent stood at a road-juncture with the Red Cross flag still flying. Whatever it had been used for, it had been stripped naked—not a cot or a bandage had been left. We cast our eyes across the green level for miles; there were all the signs of recent frenzy, but nothing stirred. It was uncanny, this sudden disappearance of men and armaments. There was fighting behind us—we could hear that. There was fighting to the right and left; but before us only the silence. We began to suspect that we had pressed on too hurriedly and were in front of our own attack.

This suspicion was strengthened when one of our own batteries, far in the rear, opened fire on us, mistaking us for the enemy. To avoid their shells, we clapped spurs to our horses and went forward for yet another mile at the gallop. Then we halted behind a cutting to consider matters. Our position was trying. We were utterly exhausted and only upheld by the excitement. We had food for neither horses nor men. The water in the men's bottles had been expended on the wounded; the horses had had nothing to drink since noon. There was very little chance of the major's keeping his promise and sending us up our rations; the battery must have moved by now and neither they nor we had any knowledge as to each other's whereabouts.

To add to our complications Tubby's arm proved to have been badly smashed by a machine-gun bullet and, though he would not own it, he was suffering intensely. The light was beginning to fail and within two hours darkness would have settled. It was absolutely essential that we should find food and water, and discover what was the military situation. If we were actually in front of our attack, then it was evident that our people had lost touch with the enemy; in which case, under the cover of night, the enemy was likely to return. If he did, we and our outfit would be killed or captured.

Tubby refused to stay with the guns and rest, so we started out in separate directions to reconnoitre. Tubby went mounted on account of his arm being in a sling; I went on foot, since thus I should afford a smaller target. Throughout the day, as our difficulties and exhaustion had increased, he had grown gayer and more reckless. He had treated his broken arm as nothing; in the presence of his gallant high spirits none of us had dared to recognise hardship. As he rode away he flung back his old jest, "How's your father?"

Several of the men, not to be outdone in this game of brave pretence, shouted after him, "He's all right, sir. Till the war ends he's got his baggy pants on."

My direction took me over to a long line of woods on the right, from which came the spiteful sound of rifles firing in volleys. The sun had begun to set; as I glanced across the plain I could see Tubby, trotting far out into a sea of shadows and greenness. I felt misgivings for his safety; we had no information as to what lay ahead. Presently I met an infantryman with a bandaged forehead, who confirmed my doubts. He told me that he and fourteen others had pressed on, keeping the enemy in sight and supposing that the rest of the advance was following.

The enemy had made a stand; it was then they had discovered that they were out of touch and unsupported. "My mates," he said, "I don't know whether they're alive or dead. They were holding out when I left; they sent me back for help. Fritzie was getting ready to counter-attack. He may be coming any moment." He looked back apprehensively and, without waiting to say more, staggered on. I reached and entered my wood.

Bullets were tearing through the leaves and branches, going by with the hiss of serpents. Beneath the shadow of the trees I found stables and a camp; but the Huns, before they had cleared out, had loaded up every particle of food and forage. Nothing but the bare buildings were left. Following a track, I came to water-troughs, but it would be impossible to lead our horses down to them while the rifle-fire lasted. On the farther edge of the wood I came across our infantry.

They were lying flat on their stomachs and crawling from point to point on their hands and knees, sniping at the enemy. They were very few in numbers, over fifty *per cent* of their force having fallen during the day. By their vigilance and the rapidity of their fire they were trying to create the impression that they were stronger than they were. I found their colonel. He was not certain, but believed they were the front-line. The tanks and the cavalry had disappeared entirely. They might be still pursuing; they might have been captured; they all might have become casualties.

At any rate, the line of these woods was the front that he intended to maintain throughout the night; so I arranged to run a telephone wire up to him and to stand to throughout the hours of darkness in case of a surprise attack. One definite piece of information I gleaned from him—that his left flank was "up in the air." Any time that the enemy discovered the fact, he could get round behind this handful of men; in the direction which Tubby had taken there was nothing between himself and the enemy.

Hurrying back through the wood I found, when I came out on the farther side, that my section had followed me. While I had been gone, the sergeants had also learnt that nothing stood between themselves and the Hun. When I asked them whether they had news of Mr. Grain they shook their heads; the last they had seen of him was an insignificant dot dwindling into the distant landscape. They had left two mounted men in the cutting to guide him on to us if he returned.

The horses were "all in" by this time from lack of water, so there was nothing for it but for some of us to take a chance and go down to the trough with buckets. I lost two of my best drivers there.

We had one piece of luck to console us. In my absence the men had run across some of our fallen cavalry and had collected sufficient oats from their feed-bags to go the rounds and sufficient rations from the haversacks of the dead to last the men.

Just as we had finished watering and feeding, we saw a tank lumbering homewards round the point of the wood through the dusk. I galloped out to meet it. The officer in charge halted and put his head out on seeing me approaching.

"Hulloa, old bean," he laughed, "what are you doing up here all on your wild lone? You know there's nobody in front."

I explained matters and asked if he had seen anyone like Tubby.

"A little fat chap with his arm in a sling?" he asked. "Yes, I saw him. I shouted to him and tried to stop him, but all he did was to ask me a silly question about my father. I don't think he was all there. He rode on towards the village from which I was escaping. It was empty when first I entered, so I waddled about for half an hour mucking things up. By that time the Huns had found out that we weren't following and they were coming back. So I skedaddled. If I were you I wouldn't go and look for your friend—Hulloa, what's that? You'd better duck!"

That was a burst of bullets, coming from a clump of trees to the left. The chap was right; the enemy was sneaking back.

I wheeled the guns about and went off at the trot to a little copse in which I had arranged with the infantry colonel to take up my position for the night. It was pitchy black when we arrived; the place stank of blood. It was already occupied by sleeping men; they did not speak to us, but we tripped over them in the darkness and felt them beside us when we lay down.

Having unlimbered our guns and got them on for line, we ran a wire up front to the colonel so as to keep in touch and open fire on the second if required. We divided our men into watches; they were wearied out, for it was many nights since they had slept. They lay down with all their equipment on, so as

159

to lose no time in the event of an alarm. The girths of the saddles were loosened, but none of the harness was removed from the horses' backs. If the enemy broke through, the first news we were likely to get would be when they were upon us. Our lives and those of the infantry might depend upon our promptitude of action.

It was just before dawn that Tubby's horse rejoined us riderless. There was blood on the saddle and the reins were broken as though the little beast had wrenched itself free by jumping back from the thing to which it had been tied. It was a broncho trick it had, which was well known to all the battery. When in our lines it was never fastened, but allowed to stand. The broken lines proved that it had been in strangers' hands; Tubby would never have tied it. When the men asked it what had happened to its master, it looked at them with quivering nostrils and frightened eyes and then, turning its intelligent head, gazed back over the way that it had come.

With the first of the daylight we discovered why it was that the men with whom we had shared the wood had been so very silent—why they had not spoken when we had tripped over them, or been disturbed when we had lain down beside them.

Sticking out of the pocket of one of them was a London daily of fairly recent date. I picked it up in mere curiosity and glanced through its pages. Then suddenly, for fear anyone should want to borrow it, I hid it away in my tunic. It contained an extraordinary story, affecting the honour of a man I loved well—an account of the police-court proceedings in the case of Mrs. Percy Dragott.

An odd way to get news of the secrets of a pal, with whom you eat and risk your life daily—by rifling the pocket of a stranger, whom you had thought to be sleeping and had discovered to be dead!

The rest of the battery caught us up this morning in our copse which we tenant with the dead. We are resting today, holding the line in depth, while the troops who were behind us yesterday, have passed through us and beyond. Far out in the blue we can catch the rapid thud of their drum-fire. With them it is, as it was with us yesterday, thirst, heroism, cruelty, magnanimity mingling in an ecstatic trance, while the August woods drip scarlet with men's triumphant carelessness of dying. From here the orchestra of murder has passed, leaving as record of its passage the brief putrescence of the earthly part of sacrifice guarded by the shadowy sunlit silence.

Is it worth it? What does it all mean, this furious display of homicidal passion? It's easy for the armchair crusaders who sit at home to prate about the glory of war. One glimpse at the landscape on which I gaze would bruise their lips with reality and wash the mountebank valour with tears from their eyes. We who have seen war for what it is, will always speak of it as the filthiest of jobs, fit only for human orang-utans or maniacs. A woman risks her life that a man may be born. It takes twenty-five long years of love to build his mind and spirit into manliness.

What glory can there be in tearing the carefully planned strength of nations barbarously limb from limb in a second? This war may have been unavoidable, but our political and journalistic prophets have no right to dress it up to appear what it is not—war is an unclean orgy of jungle-cannibals revelling in the obscenity of entrails and blood. Half the time it is not even brave; there is nothing brave in smothering a front-line with shells which are fired from miles behind the danger; there is nothing brave in overwhelming a demoralized enemy by sheer weight of numbers.

Yesterday we slaughtered men like vermin and with as little thought. We were urged on by an impelling rage, which made us almost divine in our destroying eloquence. What we did was right; the feeling I have today is only the reaction of disgust. That I should be able to feel disgust and yet go on fighting, proves more than anything else the righteousness of our cause.

We shall win the war for freedom, but at what a cost! If the British, who have already perished, were to march twenty abreast from sunrise to sunset, it would take them ten days to pass a given point. It would take the French eleven days, the Russians five weeks, the whole of the Allied dead two and a half months, and the skeletons of the fallen enemy six weeks more. If all the armies of men of whatever nations who have died fighting since August, 1914, were to march in review, twenty abreast, before the grand-stand of the living, it would take them four months to pass. This would not include the old men, women and children who have perished from disease and privation, from military brutalities, from the sinking of ships and the haphazard cruelties of shell-fire and bombs. Yet despite the tremendous thought of such a procession, the actual *pathos* of one man smashed in battle is more appalling.

Comparatively few people have seen that sight. If they had, the war would end tomorrow. The generals who plan our battles rarely see it; they are too far back. The war-correspondents who describe our battles do not see it; they collect their information second-hand at canteens, dressing-stations and army headquarters. Our civilians only read the correspondents' descriptions. So it goes—the more hands through which the news passes and the further back it travels, the more the vileness of the happening becomes misted over with lies and transmuted into something magnificent.

Each informant, in the proportion that he is removed from the terror, is the more anxious to pose as an heroic eye-witness. The only eye-witnesses are the men who do the dying, and they do not feel themselves to be heroes. They are under fire on account of the accidents of medical fitness, youth and a properly developed sense of duty. They are people of inferior rank and of no social or military consequence. They are not literary, oratorical, articulate. Because they die, the world never learns what war is like. Even though they bear charmed lives and survive, they are muzzled by army orders and the vigilance of the censor.

Not a whisper of the truth escapes. In hospital or on leave they are eager to forget; moreover, they quickly learn that the Sir Galahad misconceptions of civilians make their facts sound like the whimperings of cowards. So they strike the attitude which is required of them, pretending that there's a sporting fascination about blowing and being blown into atoms.

I glance up from my writing. Wherever my eyes wander they dwell on some shocking detail of defiled beauty or tattered flesh. From the shadow of trees and through parted grass, faces which yesterday were vivacious with health, stare vacantly at me growing green and yellow. They are more still than the sleepers of a Rip Van Winkle land. Their shoulders are hunched, their knees drawn up, their hands clenched. Beside them little piles of paper flutter or dance away like white butterflies drifted through the sunshine. The wind stoops over them like an invisible rag-picker, curiously fingering the scattered pages.

Early this morning some of the troops who passed through us to the fight, ransacked the pockets of their fallen comrades. The objects of their search were mainly matches and cigarettes, but in some cases they exchanged boots and *puttees*. I suppose they argued that you cannot rob a man who is dead; he has no further use for his possessions. Sooner or later someone is bound to rob him; that being the case, there is no one who can do it with less offence than men who are shortly to die themselves. Nevertheless it's a strange and brutal logic, for these very men may themselves be equally stark and incapable of resentment by sundown. Moreover, they showed an unnecessary callousness in their borrowing, when they scattered letters from sweethearts, wives and mothers to the four winds of heaven. In peacetimes we keep the memory of our friends alive with flowers; in war, the moment the breath has left a comrade's body he ceases to be human and becomes the victim of disrespect.

What a chamber of horrors one day's fighting has made of these woods! No human ingenuity can compete with the diabolical inventiveness of death. No two postures are alike in this array of corpses; each one strikes a different note of agony. Why should we have come so far, from Canada, Australia and the wideness of the world, to create this French landscape into such a slaughter-house? Why, above all things, should we still be willing to hand over our bodies to add one touch more to its martyred picturesqueness? We must be drunk with visions so to carve out of living flesh the image of our despotic idealism. Saints or devils, whichever we are, war has made us more than men.

My mind is full of thoughts of Tubby. He has not returned. There is no news of him. He will not return now. He may be a prisoner. He may be lying up forward wounded. He may be sprawled on the ground, like one of these pitiful waxworks by which I am surrounded. Probably we shall never know his fate. Why did he come to the war? What hidden spark of divinity kindled his spirit to a flame? He never let us inspect anything but the earthy side of his nature.

His faults, had he lived to be middle-aged, would probably have hardened into vices. He was typical of us—an ordinary, pleasant chap, a trifle specked with blackguardism, impatient of ideals and yet following in their tracks. His worst weakness was his unbalanced attitude towards women; his kindest quality that he was invariably good-tempered and generous. If he realised the possession of a soul, he never talked about it. His last recorded utterance, according to the tank-officer, was an undignified catch-phrase of the streets, "How's your father?" Yet, incredible, lovable man, he rode out wounded to die for others as simply as if he had hailed from Nazareth.

We know nothing of each other, we men who eat and sleep, and suffer, and die together. How little we know was illustrated for me by what I learnt from that newspaper, picked out of a dead man's pocket this morning.

The first I heard of a woman in Heming's life was that day on the Somme when, thinking he was about to die, he asked me to write to Mrs. Percy Bragott. From time to time after that I saw her portrait in the English illustrated weeklies and gathered that she was playing with war work, taking part in charitable theatrical performances, bazaars for the mutilated, garden-parties for the blinded, etc.,—having a thoroughly enjoyable time and acquiring a reputation for patriotic fervour.

The next occasion when her name cropped up was when the major read aloud to Heming the unconcluded account of a tragedy. In the paper which I found this morning, I read that she was on trial for murder. Mrs. Percy Dragott, it seemed, had arrived in London with no credentials several years before the outbreak of war, bringing with her an elderly husband, to whom she had been recently married, who had just retired from an appointment in the Indian Civil Service. At first by her charity, then by her beauty and finally by her brilliancy she had won for herself a place in London society.

At the end of two years her husband, having served his purpose, had died, leaving her free to take full advantage of her popularity. She was emphatically a man's woman and had found a ready welcome wherever brains were an asset, being particularly sought after by men in public life. Her little house in Mayfair, run with extravagant taste, though no one troubled to enquire where the money came from, had become a kind of salon. The names of the men to whom she had been rumoured to be about to become engaged would take two hands to reckon; they included artists, journalists, soldiers and at least one statesman.

On looking back, a fact was brought to light which had escaped notice, namely that over all the men with whom she had been associated she seemed to have spread a blight—in one way or another, after dropping her acquaintance, they had each one failed. Yet until the murder had occurred, no breath of scandal had touched her. Even now the crime would never have been discovered had not the murdered man proved to be a British secret service agent.

Colonel Barton, as he had called himself, had been introduced to her as a somewhat romantic figure. The account he had given of himself was that he had been captured at Gallipoli and had made a sensational escape from a Turkish prison-camp. For the first time she, who had earned for herself the reputation of being the coldest woman in London, seems to have been fired with passion. Whether she actually fell in love or had only feigned to do so because she scented danger, it was impossible to say. The man's case was plain; he had pretended to be infatuated with her in order that he might trap her. He had evidently learnt all that he wanted to know and was on the point of exposing her to the authorities, when he was found dead in his flat.

At first his death was taken to be an accident. It seemed that he had fainted and in falling had caught himself a heavy blow on the left temple. But when the rooms were searched, it was found that they had been already ransacked. Nothing that could be traced had been removed, but the thief had been identified as a woman by an initialled handkerchief, which she had left behind her. Moreover she had failed to discover all the papers which condemned her; lying full in sight on the desk was an unsealed, unaddressed envelope, containing the complete history which would have led to her arrest. The contention of the police was that Barton had been done to death by the popular and charitable society beauty.

Upon investigation she was proved to be a British subject in the Hun employ. Her motives for having turned traitor and spy were said to have been inspired by her resentment at the injustice of her birth; she was the illegitimate daughter of an Englishman of title, had been well-educated, kept always abroad in the care of strangers and had been given to understand through her father's lawyers that the moment she tried to hold direct communication with her father's family her income would end. How much of this Dragott knew when he married her was not certain. He was a kindly, honourable, well-born man and had arrived at an age when men attain a wise leniency of view towards social accidents. He became extremely fond of her and brought her back to England. She saw her native country for the first time in his company, and she saw it as a spy in the pay of Germany. After her husband's death, it was German money which had maintained the elegant extravagance of the little house in Mayfair.

Up to this point her story called more for sympathy than condemnation. If she, an Englishwoman, was England's enemy, it was the unkindness of English laws that had made her that. The loneliness and family ostracism of her girlhood, when combined with her more than ordinary beauty of body and brilliancy of mind, had warped her nature into a bitter desire to be revenged.

How much her husband or any of her subsequent suitors had guessed of her real occupation it was difficult to establish; but there was evidence which indicated that more than one of them had suspected. She herself had made the statement that long before her husband's death she had tried to break off her relations with Berlin, but had been compelled to continue them under threats.

Her war-philanthropies had not been entirely camouflage; in particular a hospital, which she had established in France, had been the attempt of an unquiet conscience to make atonement. But she had found it impossible to disentangle herself from the web of intrigue in which she was caught. Whatever she did, whether her intentions were good or bad, was converted into a means of gathering information for the enemy. She emphatically denied that she had had any accomplices; none of the men who had been in love with her had wilfully betrayed their official secrets. It was because she had not wished to involve others in her own tragedy that she had persistently refused all offers of marriage, earning for herself the reputation of being the coldest woman in London. Above all things she denied that she had had anything to do with Barton's death.

From the tone of the press it was evident that, in spite of the violent hatreds of war-times, a good deal of popular sympathy was felt for her. This was no doubt partly accounted for by her reckless endeavours to save her friends at the expense of incriminating herself still further. All the indiscreet conversations and confidences which had taken place across her table were being remembered and brought into the evidence. Some of the biggest and most trusted men in public life would shortly find themselves in the witness-box. Among the small fry Heming was mentioned as one of her admirers.

I'm wondering about Heming and trying to piece the little I know of his relations with her together. I'm sure he was in love with her to the point of marrying her; I believe she was in love with him to the point of confessing why she could not consent. His proposal must have taken place between the time when he was so severely wounded at Vimy and his unexpected return to the front this Spring. It's since his return that he has been so changed, so that we've all felt in our bones that he had come back for only one reason—to die.

Poor Heming, all this summer while he's been waiting for a soldier's death to solve life's complications, he must have been struggling between his instinct to protect this woman and his duty to betray her. I understand now his tenderness to Suzette and her child, who is also illegitimate.

If Heming does not know this latest development, it must be kept from him. There'll be little chance of his seeing papers so long as the offensive lasts, with its stealth and night-marches. When whatever is left of the battery marches out to rest, he may be lying quietly, like Tubby, in some deserted wood beyond all caring. Tubby's horrid little worry was quickly forgotten—in the flash of a second.

Poor Tubby, with his cheerful grin and his, "How's your father?"

I must speak to the major about Heming and get him to help me to keep him in ignorance.

Just as I had finished writing this sentence I looked up to see Suzette and Heming disappearing into the wood where our horse-lines are hidden. I don't think that there's any doubt that she's infatuated with him; wherever he goes, though her feet stay still, her eyes and her heart follow. She's still a woman in her every movement, despite her Tommy's uniform. And Heming, what are his feelings? Is he using her as a means to drug memory? Or does she restore to him a chivalrous belief that he was in danger of losing?

He never commits himself and rarely speaks to her except to give orders. Queer motives urge men to become heroes. What stories we should have if every man told honestly the reasons that sent him here! One has committed a sin; another has entrusted his heart to the wrong woman. They ride out into the hell of judgement day laughing, and perish insolently, that in their last moments they may appear again magnificent to themselves.

CHAPTER 22

Awaiting New Orders

It's midnight. We're still in the copse. We believe we are to take part in a new attack tomorrow, but have received no orders as yet.

I am squatting on the ground beneath a low tent made of Hun greatcoats and sacking pinned together. On one side of me, more than half filling the tiny space, the major lies asleep; on the other is a shaded candle and the telephone which keeps us in touch with brigade. Every quarter of an hour the brigade-signallers buzz me to make sure that the line is holding up. Every now and then I draw the flimsy patchwork of the roof nearer together lest any light should be escaping.

Ever since darkness settled, the Hun planes have been bombing our back areas, getting after our horse-lines, ammunition dumps and infantry concentrations. When one of them has scored a direct hit on a dump, all the country within the radius of half a mile is flooded with a pulsating wave of red. While it lasts, no movement remains hidden from the watchers in the sky; a man stands out as distinctly as a tower. In the welter of blackness the glow of a cigarette, a match struck however furtively, the leakage of light from a bivouac, show up as significantly as beacon-fires. The human-eagles got after us in fine style two hours ago, coming so close that we had to ride our horses bareback into the night, pursued from the air not only by bombs but also by machine-guns.

Now all our men who are not on duty are trying to snatch

what rest they can before another disturbance starts. There always is another, and a next and a next. The Hun airmen, having exhausted their supply of bombs, have flown back to replenish. They're due to return almost any minute and will do their best again to pick up our scent. If we don't attack tomorrow, we can't stay here, now that we have been spotted.

I'm appallingly sleepy and am scribbling chiefly in an effort to keep my eyes from closing. They feel as if they had been filled with dust; I have to wedge my lids up with my fingers to prevent them from falling. I can well understand how sentries drop off at their posts, despite the knowledge that they are committing a shooting offence. It's strange to reflect that in civil life no money could have persuaded us to put up with one tithe of our dis-comforts, let alone with our dangers super-added. If we get back to a world of sheeted beds, all former necessities will seem forever luxuries.

Earlier in the evening I told the major about Heming. He agreed with me that we must do our best to prevent him from learning about Mrs. Dragott. The major was quite frank in the expression of his opinion. "There are some kinds of messes you can live down," he said; "the results of them may make you even stronger to face life. My kind of mess is a case in point. I go home on leave, expecting to marry my girl, and find that not only has she jilted me, but that she has the cheek to compel me to save her face by attending her wedding to another chap. Of course I had a lucky escape; if that was the sort she was, life with her would have been unbearable.

At the same time the experience has crippled my belief in myself and, up to a point, my faith in women generally. I'm not particular whether I come out of the war—that's the way I feel at present. But on one thing I am determined: I'll prove to her before I die that she backed the wrong horse and was a rotten bad guesser. I'll take every chance and try to win every decoration. When the war ends, if I'm still above ground, I'll succeed all I can and collar a girl a thousand times more kind than she ever dreamt of being. So I suppose instead of smashing me, she's really helped to make me. Now with Heming it's quite different. He may not know it, but he's still in love with his woman. By her method of refusing him, she made herself romantic to him. She pushed him from her when she confessed she was a spy; but at the same time she roused his pity and drew him to her.

By no stretch of imagination can he ever win her, neither can he ever quite lose her. He'll be lucky if he isn't recalled to bear witness against her; if he is, he will smudge his own honour. And as for her, if she isn't shot, she'll certainly get penal servitude. The most fortunate thing that could happen to him is that he should fall in action. If we can help it, he must never hear of this tragedy. We've a month of hard fighting ahead of us. Many of us will go west before the days grow much shorter. I hope for his sake he's one of them. I shan't try to prevent his going."

"And what about Suzette?" I asked.

He returned my question, "Well, and what about her?"

"We've no right to have her with us," I said. "She might get killed."

"And if she does," the major took me up, "that wouldn't be the worst calamity that could befall her. Death's not the final tragedy we used to think it; very often it's the new start. Her life was probably gray enough before we found her—a peasant girl, who had been used by men and would probably be used by men to the end of the chapter. What kind of a career has she ahead of her if we throw her down now? There's nothing but devastated country behind us.

If I told her tomorrow that she'd got to buzz off, where would she go or who would care what happened? No, she's going to stay with us; and if she comes through it all, we'll make ourselves responsible for her and take her back with us to Canada. I tell you what it is, the more I see of that girl, the more grateful I am that she's with us. She's restored my ideal of women. You think I'm talking like an ass, no doubt; but from Heming down, there's not an unmarried man in the battery who's not more or less in love with her. No, my boy, until we've been found out and have received direct orders to get rid of her, Suzette stops."

"And Bully Beef?" I asked.

"And Bully Beef," he answered. "He can always be left behind with the transport when we're in action. Old Dan Turpin will look after him. He considers him his own kid already."

I've been sitting here thinking over this conversation, and especially over one sentence, "Death's not the final tragedy; very often it's the new start." Those words really explain our indifference in the face of shell-fire and torture. We no longer fear the separation of the spirit from the body. We don't regard the separation as extinction; we view it with quiet curiosity and suspect that it may only mean beginning afresh. Perhaps we're exceptional in our battery, inasmuch as there are so many who would welcome the opportunity to begin afresh. Tubby certainly must be glad of it; going on the way he was, the noble part of him would never have had a chance.

This war has made so many of us aware of a nobility which we never knew we possessed. We're a little afraid that we shall lose it, if we live through to the corpulent days of peace. We would rather go west at the moment when we are acting up to our most decent standards. It's odd, but when threatened by death, it's the fear of life that assails us. The dread of old age grips us by the throat; the terror of old temptations, which of late we have been too athletic in soul to gratify, confronts us. The gray, unheroic monotony of unmerited failures and unworthy successes daunts us. We dread lest when war ends, the old grasping selfishnesses may reassert themselves. Today we have the opportunity to go out like Vikings, perishing in a storm. To live a few years longer only to shuffle off, will not be rewarding.

At this point I have to leave off. A runner has just come in bringing us word that we are to be prepared to push forward at dawn.

CHAPTER 23

Death Corner

The major's opportunity to prove his girl "a rotten bad guesser" came sooner than we expected. I shouldn't be at all surprised to see Charlie Wraith with a V. C. ribbon on his breast before many days are out. He hardly fills the bill for the popular conception of a hero, with his little bandy-legs and his deathly pallor; but it's what a chap is that counts. This is how his opportunity occurred.

It was 6 a. m. when we moved off. We had been harnessed up and ready, awaiting our final orders for two hours. When they did arrive, they came with a rush, as per usual; we were scarcely given sufficient time to complete our march before we were required to be in action. Measuring off the distance on the maps which accompanied the orders, we discovered that to be in time for the attack it would be necessary for us to travel all the way at the hard trot. The major went on ahead of us to reconnoitre the position, leaving Heming to lead the battery.

Our direction lay across the plateau from which we had been turned back by enemy fire on the day we lost Tubby. The enemy had been pushed far back now; the roads were so thronged by our own transport that we had to forsake beaten tracks and take our chances across country. There was always the danger that we might mistake landmarks which we believed we had recognised from our maps, and so lose time; there was also the risk that in the open we might be held up by uncut wire-entanglements.

It was a gorgeous morning, blue and golden, with a touch of

ice in the air. Over turf and woodlands, as far as eye could search, the dew had flung a silver mesh.

The sky was almost without a cloud; tumbling through its depths, like eels in a tank, aeroplanes looped and wriggled. The landscape was one continuous chain of island-woods, each one of which had been a machine-gun fortress of the enemy. We were told that in some of them the enemy were still fighting, though they knew that they were hopelessly marooned and that our advance had swept on many miles ahead. Under the shadow of trees villages were dotted about, most of them possessing a tall spired church.

From what we could see in the hurry of our passage, every human habitation had been laid level with the ground. It was impossible to believe that this destruction was the result of British shells, since our artillery had been too far behind to do the damage. It must have been the deliberate demolition of the Hun when he knew that he had to retire. In his retreat he had stolen everything that he had not destroyed. No food, furniture or livestock were left; all the inhabitants had been carried off captive.

The position we were looking for was in the neighbourhood of a crossroads, unpropitiously marked "Death Corner" on the map. It was at the entrance to a village which our infantry were rumoured to have captured at dawn; whether they had captured it or, having captured it, had been able to hold it, we did not know for certain.

Some parts of our journey we had to go at the walk on account of the roughness of the ground, but most of the way we went at the trot. As the sun grew stronger, our horses broke into a foam of sweat. Men and animals were wildly excited. This was soldiering as depicted by battle-artists and recruiting posters—a very different job from the tedious, wakeful misery of night-marches. All the officers and mounted N. C. O's had picked up swords from the fallen cavalry. A good many of the men had armed themselves with revolvers which they had salvaged from the dead. We didn't know how close we were going to get to the enemy, but we had hopes.

What struck us most forcibly, especially as we drew nearer to the thunder of the guns, was the lightness with which our line was held. One saw no supporting troops; it seemed as though we had thrown every last man into the actual fighting. We began to apprehend why we had to keep on attacking: the Hun was falling back on his reserves; if we let him halt to regain his breath he would take the offensive. Were that to happen, our retreat might prove just as precipitate as our advance.

We were riding now through the batteries which had leap-frogged us yesterday. They were firing away like mad. The air was shaken with rapid concussions. It was impossible to make oneself heard; all our commands had to be given by signals. On ahead things looked pretty hot; the ground kept spouting up in fountains of dust and flame. Increasingly the enemy retaliation was finding us out. We clapped spurs to our horses and broke into a gallop.

Out of the cloud of drifting smoke our little major emerged, signalling to us to follow him. He led us on clear beyond the other batteries, till we were almost treading on the heels of our infantry. We had scarcely downed trail, when he gave us our aiming-point and directions, and had us tearing off four rounds a minute. I looked at my wristwatch. Pretty work! We had arrived just in time and had got into action on the second. As our teams trotted back to our temporary wagon-lines, a hail of shells came over, wounding several of the men and horses.

There was precious little information as to what had happened or was happening. Our infantry had captured the town immediately in front of us and were preparing to go forward behind our barrage to capture the next town which lay ahead. Everybody said that we had insufficient tanks for the task and that the enemy was making a determined stand. How much of this was conjecture and how much fact, nobody could assert positively.

There was a feeling of tension and anxiety. No one was quite certain what he was expected to accomplish. Our own fear was that in firing without more exact information we might be killing our own men. The major himself determined to go forward to ascertain the true condition of affairs. While he was gone, Heming returned from the wagon-lines, bringing with him two Hun field-guns he had found, so making us into an eight-gun battery.

We had been firing for about half an hour when a mounted signaller, sent back by the major, rode up. He reported that the attack had been only partially successful, owing to the tremendous concentration of enemy machine-guns, which lay hidden in the wheat-fields between the two towns. Another attack was to take place within the hour; it was necessary that the battery should move up in order that our support might be more immediate and effective. The signaller added that the major was at Death Corner, in full sight of the enemy and that his groom had been killed within five minutes of his arrival there.

We hooked in and started off by a mud-track. The mud-track was strewn on either side by men and horses, newly dead. Some of them we recognised as people who had passed us while we had been in action. The enemy shells were sweeping the track for all the world as though a gigantic hose were playing down its length. Now they would spray this part of it, then lift a hundred yards and spray that. Ahead of us stretched a billowy level of wheat-fields; to the right lay Rouvroy, the town which we had captured; at right angles to the track and passing in front of Rouvroy ran a road, which was clearly indicated above the wheat by a straight line of splintered trees.

The point where the track met the road was Death Corner. It looked as unhealthy a spot as one could well imagine; everything was rocking in a whirlwind of explosions. Three hundred yards short of the corner we swung off to the left and came into action. Over the short distance which separated the battery from the major we ran in a telephone wire. From where he was and indeed from any point on the high road, the entire battle-field lay exposed and, on its furthest edge, the entrenched town of Fouquescourt which it was essential we should possess.

The major had arranged with the infantry that, at a given

signal, we would at once open at an intense rate of fire and that behind our shells the advance against the town should commence. We had been firing for, perhaps, five minutes, when we received orders from our brigade headquarters, which were well in rear of us, to stop. The major, watching from his point of vantage, saw that all of a sudden our advancing riflemen were left unprotected. He called up to know what was the matter and at once ordered us to go on. For the next two hours we purposely let our line to brigade go down so that we might be out of touch and left unhampered to do our work.

And what a two hours those next two hours were! The Hun was putting up the fight of his life. All through the three thousand yards of wheatfields which separated Rouvroy from Fouquescourt wire-entanglements and machine-gun nests had been constructed. You could not see them for the grain, and did not know they were there until you were upon them. In the first advance which had failed, our men had walked straight into the traps and most of their officers had been shot down. In the second, which we had come up close to support, our men had wriggled their way forward and reached Fouquescourt, only to find that they were cut off and had left the enemy in the wheat behind them.

In losing time we were giving the enemy his chance. He was bringing his guns up and getting them into better positions; every hour his artillery fire was becoming better directed and growing more intense. His airmen were regaining their courage, flying in leaps and bounds like great grasshoppers just above our heads, and picking off our men with machine-gun fire. We had to keep two Lewis guns mounted on the flanks of our battery to drive them off.

Things had reached a pretty desperate pass, everyone fighting without proper information and in many cases without leadership, when suddenly, silently and unheralded, out of the woods behind us appeared a cloud of cavalry. They drew up, as if on parade, about four hundred yards to our left flank and in line with ourselves. They were instantly spotted by a Hun plane, which flew to and fro over them, dropping bombs. He was so busily engaged that he did not notice one of our chaps swooping down on him. When he did see him, there was nothing for it but to escape. Then followed a wild chase; our chap hovering like a hawk on top and driving the Hun lower and lower towards the ground.

Of a sudden the Hun burst into flames and shot downwards like a torch. But before he was caught he must have signalled back the cavalry target to his gunners, for right into the midst of the waiting horsemen the shells began to fall. Their courage was superb, the courage of the horses equalling that of the men. From the distance at which we watched, it was exactly like seeing rocks flung into a pond—only the rocks were high explosives and the pond was made up of living flesh. We saw the splash of bodies tossed high into the air, the ripple of horsemen reining back, and then the patient orderly reforming of their ranks.

A trumpet sounded. At a walk, and then at a gentle trot, a hundred men rode up on to the high-road and vanished into the sea of yellow on the other side. Then a hundred more. Then a hundred more, till none but those who could not rise were left. As each little company was displayed to the enemy, the high-road was swept with bullets as with pelting hail. Riders crumpled in their saddles; horses reared themselves up, pawing at the air and toppled over backwards.

The survivors paid no heed to the agony which would certainly be theirs within the next few seconds; unhurriedly, keeping cool and using their heads, they set spurs to their horses and danced away to trample the machine-guns and clear a way for the infantry, or to die in the attempt. How many of them came back we did not count, but most of them found a grave in the sea of yellow.

The man at the telephone was beckoning to me. "The major wants you to speak with him," he said.

"Hulloa! hulloa! That you, major?"

"Is that you, Chris?"

"Yes."

"Is there anyone you can leave with the guns?"

"here's Edwine, Sir."

"Then come up to where I am at once."

I handed over the battery and went forward. At Death Corner I was met by a sight which I shall not easily forget. In the middle of the crossroads the dead lay in mounds. Many of them were men whom I recognised. The place was strewn with horses. The first to catch my eyes was old Fury, the major's rusty charger; his hind-legs had been shot away from under him and he sat with his front-legs thrust out like poles, balancing himself and swaying his head. Pressed flat behind a tree I saw the major, peering out across the waving corn, where the cavalry were charging death at the gallop. Crouching low and dodging the shells, I gained his place of hiding.

"Some picnic, isn't it?" were his first words. He was as happy and excited as if he were the spectator of a gigantic football match. How he had been able to survive at Death Corner for so long was a marvel. I looked at the picnic. All I could see was men creeping back on their hands and knees, riderless horses writhing and drowning in the sea of yellow, stranded tanks, smouldering heaps marking the spots where aeroplanes had crashed incandescent as comets and, across the plain of wheat, a wall of fire where our shells were falling and columns of suffocating smoke were curling above the funeral pyres of towns.

"Some picnic, all right," I said. The major laughed at me out of the corner of his eyes. " It's the real thing—open warfare, what we always wanted. See here, Chris, I've collected some of these infantry chaps; their officers have been nearly all wiped out. I'm going to lead them forward to clean up some of those enemy machine-gun nests. They've got to be cleaned up, because they're cutting us off from our troops who are in Fouquescourt. God knows what's happening up there. Someone's got to fight his way through and find out. I want you to stop here and watch for any messages I send back."

His eye caught Fury. "I can't leave him like that."

At the risk of his life he dodged across the open space to

where his old companion sat swaying his head forlornly. I saw him pat the velvet neck and then fumble for his revolver. He looked at the revolver and then at the horse. He came back to me slowly, "I can't. You do it when I'm gone."

Along the edge of the wheat the infantry were lying waiting for him; they were the stragglers and survivors of the first two attacks. As he reached them he fell on his hands and knees and crawled away, while they followed him at intervals through the golden stalks.

Had the Huns seen him at that moment, they would not have considered him an object of terror, under-sized and wizened as he was. But it was Charlie Wraith, despite his physical deficiencies, who put heart into defeated men that day and by his magnificent contempt for death forced a way into Fouquescourt to the support of troops which had become isolated. How many enemy strongholds he bombed out he alone knows, and he refuses to tell. The men whom he led cannot tell, for most of them are dead. He had always yearned to kill Germans face to face, so he must have had a time entirely satisfactory and satisfying. It wasn't his job as an artilleryman; but, as he said in excusing himself afterwards, it was a dirty job and with most of the infantry officers gone west, there was no one else to do it.

He got severely strafed on his return for having left his battery, which he ought to have been commanding. Then news began to come in of what he had actually accomplished and how it was he who had flashed back the reports which had enabled the front to be consolidated. He's been recommended for the V. C. and it looks as though he would get it. So he's attained the desire nearest to his heart; he's healed his wounded pride and will be able to prove to the girl who flung him down that her knowledge of human arithmetic was faulty.

CHAPTER 24

Title

We are still in the neighbourhood of Death Corner. It looks as though the attack has been pressed as far as it can go at this point. The whole of Fouquescourt is now in our hands, but beyond that lies Fransart and the railroad, which the enemy is holding heavily. To the south of us the French are trying to turn the enemy's flank of Noyon, but apparently with little success, for the resistance in front of us grows stiffer rather than less. The Hun is a long way from being beaten yet. Whatever may be the morale of his rank and file, his storm-troops never fought better. For two days after we had surrounded Fouquescourt there were machine-gunners who still refused to surrender and kept up a running scrap from house to house, causing us many casualties and much annoyance.

Every twenty-four hours we had to shift our guns owing to the Hun aerial activity. By day the enemy airmen spot us; under cover of night they return to bomb us. They have not scored any direct hits on our guns yet, thanks to our precautions in changing our positions every nightfall, but they have made us pay heavily in the loss of men. With so much shifting and changing it is not possible to build any overhead protection; the most we can do is to scoop holes in the ground of sufficient depth to hide us from the splinters. Next night we have to scoop fresh holes and spread our blankets somewhere else.

Owing to the precariousness of the way in which our front is held we have to be on duty all the time. At night we never dare to undress, nor even to remove our boots. This is not like the old days, when we had an elaborate system of trenches and a wide No Man's Land between ourselves and the enemy; today we have outposts dotted here and there, and a thin line of riflemen strung out through ditches and woods. In a moving battle one is never quite certain where our country ends and the Hun's commences. If we were for a minute to relax our vigilance, we might be overwhelmed. But the vigilance when combined with the bombing and the shelling is very wearing.

The weather has become unusually hot. The men go about stripped to the waist and dripping with sweat. We left all our surplus baggage behind before the offensive started, so there are few of us who have more than one change of underwear. The result is that all the time we feel prickly and dirty. We would give a month's pay for a plunge in a river and a chance to clean ourselves. Try as we may to prevent it, already a number of the men are developing skin-diseases and nearly all of them are verminous. With the constant wearing of our boots, the feet of most of us are getting blistered and sore.

One of our gun-detachments made a lucky find, which has caused them to be the envy of the battery. In what had been a Hun officers' mess they found a quantity of woman's lingerie, all of the very daintiest—pink silk finery, with baby ribbons and much lace. They at once discarded their army shirts and now lend a touch of humour to our landscape as they fire their gun in their filmy attire.

The heat has caused the carcases of the dead horses to decompose more quickly than usual; they lie indecently throughout the wheatfields and roads like huge inflated bagpipes with their legs sticking woodenly in the air. For miles the atmosphere is tainted with the nauseating stench of decaying flesh. No one has the time or the energy for burying them; even our human dead have in very many cases not yet been accorded the common kindness of a grave. We are all too tired to form funeral parties and the risk of exposing one's self is too great. All our movements have to take place under the cover of darkness; it is then that our ammunition is sent up. The Hun is perfectly aware of this; he keeps every road and suspected battery-position, with all its approaches, under constant bombardment from sundown to well after midnight.

Our rations, as may be imagined, are of the very plainest, consisting for the most part of bully beef, tea, and hard tack. To light fires to cook anything is dangerous; the smoke would give us away in a second. We have outrun our lines of communication. Our railhead is many miles behind. Everything has to be brought up to the battle area by motor-transport, across roads which the enemy did his best to destroy in his flight. We are entirely out of tobacco and cigarettes. Our only remaining smokes are Hun cigars, which we have found in abandoned billets or in the pockets of the dead.

It would have been normal to have supposed that in an advance of these dimensions we should have captured enough booty to have kept ourselves supplied. Where we are now was the Hun's back-country a few days ago, to which his troops marched out to rest. His canteens were here, his workshops and hospitals. There were plenty of French civilians still in possession of these houses; the gardens and fields were under cultivation. Our advance was so unexpected and rapid that it gave him hardly any warning of our advent; and yet he contrived to strip everything and to carry it off in his wagons. Even the gardens are bare; nothing but the crops in the fields are left. The only fresh meat which any of us have had has been supplied us by our veterinary sergeant, who holds that horse-flesh is a perfectly healthy diet if you take only the best cuts. There are plenty of wounded horses wandering about, of no further service to the army.

War has certainly taught us one thing: that we all have a far greater power of endurance than we guessed. Here we are, having put up with every kind of hardship, having experienced every kind of shock, having lived with horror as a daily companion, having gone without sleep, without proper food or anything approaching cleanliness, and yet we are happy and cheerfully prepared for as much more punishment as may be allotted.

The extraordinary cheerfulness of our men, the kind of schoolboy attitude they take up towards war, as though it were no more than a tremendous lark, is illustrated by the glee they displayed in firing the two whizz-bangs which Heming brought up to us when we were attacking Fouquescourt. I suppose they derived a grim satisfaction from pelting the enemy with his own shells. To have two more guns to serve meant that everybody had to do considerably more work. Besides the actual work of serving them, there was the added labour of hunting up and collecting the Hun ammunition which was scattered throughout the countryside. They did it all without a grumble, preferring to regard the undertaking as a joke at the enemy's expense.

Yesterday we received an order that all captured ordnance had to be drawn back to a special park, some ten miles to the rear. When our men heard that, they went out and gathered together six hundred rounds per gun and spent the night in pooping them off into the enemy back-country just as fast as they could load and fire. Funny chaps! They won't be so keen on working overtime when once they get back to their labour unions.

By the way, Suzette has just communicated to us an interesting fact about herself. She asked to be paraded before the major, as though she were actually a Tommy instead of a civilian girl. In the queer broken English which she has picked up from our men, she told us that this was her country before the war came and she had to flee from it. Her home was in Fransart, which is the next town which we shall have to attack. She wanted to let us know this because she thought her knowledge of the district might be of value. And then came what was probably her real motive for asking to be paraded; a request that she might be allowed to accompany the next officer and party of signallers going up front.

"But why? What for?" the major questioned.

"Eet was my 'ome," she said. "I wish zo much to zee eet before zee guns ———." She puffed out her cheeks and then emptied them with an explosive sound. "Before zay make eet all flat."

At first the major refused her emphatically. But the major has a soft place for Suzette; I'm not at all sure that he is not just as much in love with her as Heming. For some time I've had the feeling of a growing hidden rivalry between the two men—hidden because, being friends, they are ashamed to acknowledge rivalry. And then again, neither of them is willing to own her attraction. She has no right to be here. Were it discovered that the reason for her presence in a fighting unit was the major's or the captain's affection, the affair would wear a very different aspect in the eyes of not only the higher authorities, but also of the men in the battery itself. Compelled by her pleading, the major has promised her that on the first quiet day he will allow her to accompany one of us up front. In granting her request I think he is ill-advised. But it is clear to me now that, were she to make any request of him, however mad, he would not be able to withstand her.

As I look back, I am amazed that I have been so blind; I can remember incidents and chance phrases, insignificant in themselves, which pieced together prove beyond a doubt that the major has been in love with her from the very first. A topsy-turvy world! Nothing really matters when you may be blown into eternity any second. All I hope is that no one else has noticed.

Charlie Wraith on that day at Death Corner, laughing like a boy playing pirates! It's now plain what he was doing: he was winning the admiration of Suzette.

CHAPTER 25

Bully Beef is Lost

During the last two days I have seen the best bit of fighting of the entire war. As a rule an attack is a big sprawling affair, the whole of which no one can foresee, and the whole of which in all its details no single person can command. Everyone sets out with general instructions; but the variations in the methods by which those instructions are carried out depend on personal initiative and chance. For the first time I was in an attack every phase of which one could follow up and watch. If a moving-picture man had been there, he could have made his fortune. From first to last the entire performance was stage-set and capable of being focussed.

I was sent up forward to do liaison work with the battalion which was holding the line in front of Fouquescourt. Everything was quiet and no attack was contemplated, so Suzette had her way and was allowed to accompany me. I did not much relish having the responsibility of a girl with me in what was practically the front-line, though nobody by looking at her could have guessed that she was a girl. Her appearance was that of a slightly built boy, who was probably two years below the military age; but there was nothing to arouse suspicion in that, for many of our Tommies have obviously increased their age in order to get themselves into the army. She accompanied me ostensibly as a telephonist in my signalling party.

Battalion headquarters were situated in a deep trench, which crossed the road which runs between Fouquescourt and Fransart. This road was raked day and night by hostile fire. The trench itself was anything but a pleasant spot. The moment one poked his head up to look over the top a bullet would whizz by; Hun snipers were everywhere and quite close up. Suzette's idea in accompanying me had been to get a glimpse of Fransart before it was flattened by shells; but apart from the snipers this was impossible, for the fields sloped up into a ridge which hid all but the tops of the village trees from the trench where we were. This being the case there was not much sense in allowing her to remain in a place of danger, so I made up my mind to send her back to the battery with the runner who would carry down my situation report at nightfall.

I had never had much talk with Suzette; that afternoon as I sat in the hot sun-baked trench I got a glimpse of her mind for the first time. The rest of my party were sprawled out on their backs, trying to make up for broken nights, so we were quite by ourselves.

"Suzette," I said, "why do you follow us? It isn't a happy sort of life. Surely somewhere you must have friends."

She shrugged her shoulders ever so slightly, "My friends! Zay was all in Fransart. You are my friends now."

I tried to get her to outline to me what had happened to her since the start of the war, but she wasn't to be drawn out on that point.

"Ze Germans, zay was not nice," she said; "zay killed my mother over zare."

It appeared that her mother had kept pigeons in the loft of their cottage. When the Germans discovered that the birds had rings on their legs, they had suspected that they were intended for the carrying of messages, and her old mother had been led out and shot. She herself had escaped through their outposts and regained the unconquered territory. What had happened between the time of her escape and our finding her she passed over in a phrase, "Eet was cold and un'appy, and zen you were kind."

I found that what she really preferred to talk about was her girlhood, before calamity had touched her; so let her talk on. It was over there in Hallu Wood, from which the sniping was coming, that she had gone each spring with the village children to gather primroses. It was through these fields, where corpses were now lying, that she used to walk with her pail at milking-time. She peopled the battlefield with ghosts, recreating all the peasant ways of life that the ferocity of war had terminated. She made me see the old priest in his rusty black skirt and round felt hat, going down the lanes between the little cottages. She made me see the pool in the brook where her mother used to kneel with the village women, singing and banging the linen white against the stones. But most of all she made me see herself— Suzette, with the gold-brown plaits, whom all the boys used to follow with their eyes, before there was any Bully Beef or any hint of catastrophe in the world.

The 'phone tinkled, breaking the spell, and the telephonist on duty called to let me know that I was wanted by the major.

"Hulloa, sir, I was going to have called you up. I'm sending Suzette back. There is nothing for her to see up here."

"Don't send her back—not yet." The major's voice sounded abrupt and agitated.

"But why ?"

"Here's why. Bully Beef is lost and we don't want her to know until we've found him."

"Lost, but"

"Yes, lost. I know what you are going to say; that he can't have gone far and must have been picked up by some other unit. The fact is, however, that he's as completely vanished as if the ground had opened and swallowed him. Keep her with you until we've made a proper search. We may not have to tell her."

That night instead of returning with the runner to the battery, Suzette stayed with us in the front-line. When night had fallen and the snipers could no longer see her, she sat on the lip of the trench, staring out into the darkness towards Fransart. Once she pointed to a lone tree on the ridge, saying that she could see the village from there and asking me to allow her to go forward; but the enemy patrols were likely to be abroad, so I had to deny her. Several times I heard her sigh heavily and more than once I could have sworn that tears glistened in her eyes. She was realising all that she had lost. But how much she had lost even she did not know as yet, for every time I phoned back to the battery and questioned I received the same answer; there was no news of her child.

At the front men are missing very often for weeks before you find a trace of them. They stray into the enemy lines. They get wounded by a chance shell. Their nerve fails them at the moment when they have accomplished some heroic act and they desert. We had one man who brought in a wounded officer at the risk of his life and was recommended for a decoration. Then it was discovered that the man could not be found. When he was found, he was awarded the D. C. M. for valour and court-martialed for the cowardice of desertion. We never give up hope when a man goes missing until he is proved to be dead. But with a civilian it is different; there are no army records through which to trace and report them. Were Bully Beef found killed, it would be nobody's business. At the front one's responsibility extends no further than to the men in khaki.

Next morning on enquiring across the 'phone, I was told that they had picked up a rumour: a child had been seen on the road between the wagon-lines and Death Corner. If that were so, it would mean that Bully Beef had wandered out of the wagon-lines in the direction of the battery in search of his mother. He had come up once or twice to the battery-position with the ammunition-wagons, and would have a vague idea of the way. Seeing that he had not arrived at the battery, it was likely that he had gone past it; in which case he must be somewhere in the wheatfields between Death Corner and Fourquescourt. A detail of men were out searching for him, led by Big Dan.

Then something arose which swung my thoughts clean away from this personal anxiety. To the south of us drum-fire had been pounding away all morning; we guessed that the French had been going after Noyon once again. At one o'clock we got a sudden intimation that within two hours we must capture Fransart and, if possible, the railroad which lay beyond. This left no time for the working out of the usual detailed plans for artillery co-operation. Moreover, we were too far forward to dare to send our instructions back by telephone; the Hun listening-machines would pick up our conversations and the enemy would be forewarned.

We had to make out a rough barrage-table and run it back to the guns by messenger. When that was done it was necessary that I and my party should go forward to the jumping-off point with the infantry, since the ridge in front blocked the view of the area where the fighting was to take place. Suzette volunteered to accompany my party, and since I had far too few signallers for a show and no time to obtain more, I was compelled to accept her. Leaving one man in the trench to watch for our messages, we struck out along the Fouquescourt-Fransart road and commenced to lay in wire to the point from which we proposed to observe the fight.

It was a brilliantly hot afternoon; all the parched landscape seemed to shift and quiver in the dancing haze. One's clothes rasped the flesh like sandpaper and one's eyes were blinded by perspiration. We made little progress with the laying of our wire, for every few minutes we had to go back to mend a break caused by shell-fire. At last we abandoned the idea of keeping in touch with the rear by telephone and determined to rely on visual signalling. We passed the ruined village of Fouquescourt on our right. It was seething in a cloud of smoke; the shriek of bursting shells was like the wild applause of waves breaking on a rock-bound coast.

We abandoned the road and bore over towards the left, till we came to an old Hun trench, which ran straight up to Fransart and passed near to the lone tree on the ridge, from which we intended to signal back our messages. As we stole crouching between its shallow banks, we noted how our chaps had flung away the heavier part of their equipment; it was strewn with haversacks, Mill's bombs and tins of bully. Then, when we almost thought that we had advanced too far, we came across them. They were kneeling close together, panting like over-driven animals, their bayonets gleaming thirstily in the fierce sunshine. Many of them were reinforcements who had never been in battle before—men who had been sent to replace the heavy casualties of our encounters. Their faces were haggard with the struggle against terror and they trembled as they waited for our guns to open fire.

One could pick out the veterans among them at a glance by their fatalistic carelessness. Having posted a signaller with flags and a lamp, I pushed forward to where the company commander was waiting to lead the advance. He was just on the crest, from where one could look down on the approaches to Fransart. The village itself was still hidden from sight, but one could see the little country road, running through fields straight and white as an arrow from Fouquescourt, and crossing the road a line of apple trees. It looked very sleepy and innocent. One would scarcely have been surprised to have seen blue-clad peasants rise out of the grass and commence to sharpen their scythes. There was no hint of murder and strife; the suspense of the crouching men behind us struck a false note of melodrama. The company commander consulted his wristwatch, counting off the minutes.

He turned to me. "How many more do you make it?"

"Six minutes more to go," I replied.

"What are you doing when the show has started?"

"I follow you up," I said, "and keep you in sight. If you want to send any runners back, you'll find some of my signallers in this trench."

Then we again fell to watching the quiet country with a kind of wonder, counting off the minutes and the seconds.

There were only two minutes left when the infantry-officer jerked my elbow excitedly, "Good God, look at that!"

"At what?"

"Get your glasses out, man, they're better than mine. That thing over there, moving towards the apple-trees down the road."

I picked up the object with my naked eye when he pointed. It was a mere speck, creeping very slowly. It might have been a man crawling, only it was hardly big enough. Our riflemen already had their sights trained on it and their fingers on the triggers, awaiting the order to fire. I raised my glasses. What I saw was a child, with chubby legs, short skirts and long hair to the middle of his back like a girl's. His face was streaky with crying, and he kept digging his knuckles into his eyes. Through the glasses he looked so near that I could have touched him by reaching out my hand. It was horrible to see him out there, where in little over a minute our own shells would be falling.

Our little Bully Beef, going in search of his mother! There wasn't one of us who wouldn't have given up his life to restore him to her, and we were powerless to draw him back. The rifles were lowered as the word was whispered round; we watched his progress in fascinated suspense.

Suddenly, rising out of a ditch behind him, came another figure—Big Dan's. Big Dan, who had promised to take care of him in his mother's absence! He leapt up and ran towards the enemy lines down the ribbon of white road. He must have called to Bully Beef, for we saw the child turn and fling out his arms at recognising him. Dan picked him up, holding him tight against his breast, and stood there hesitating, waiting for the enemy to take their revenge. I could almost hear him singing defiantly, in his deep base voice,

Old soldiers never die.
They simply fade away.

Then a hundred yards in front, out of the apparent emptiness a Hun stood up waving a handkerchief; beside the Hun were a dozen rifles all pointing in Dan's direction. He moved forward, with the child's face looking back across his shoulder. As the first of our shells fell, he stepped down and was lost to sight in the German trench. Like a squall at sea our barrage descended and everything was blotted out.

I turned to the signaller who was nearest to me, "Where is

Suzette?"

"Behind the next traverse, sir."

"She did not see? She does not know?"

"She doesn't know, sir."

"Then until it is all over we must not tell her."

It took five minutes for the enemy retaliation to come back. It burst like a hurricane along the ridge and along the shallow hiding place in which we were. No man could hide there for long. The only safety was to get either in front of it or behind it. The company-commander gave the signal to advance. With the men running and crouching low, the river of bayonets streamed past me. Like a trickling stream, I watched their silver gleaming grow more distant above the tall rank grass which lined the lip of the trench. God knows to what fate they were going or how many of those splendidly fashioned men would remain unbroken by sunset. For myself, I had other things to think about.

My job was to keep the attack in sight and to be sure that my chain of signallers was in touch with the rear, so that I could get my orders through for the directing of fire. To keep the attack in sight it was necessary to push on nearer to Fransart, so I took Suzette and one man with me, leaving the rest of my party strung out behind. Where the apple-trees crossed the road, I saw our men leap out of the trench and start at the run across the open. Instantly a withering fire was brought to bear on them from a little village in advance and over to the right, which we had been informed had been in our hands since morning. They began to go down like nine-pins, pitching forward into the dust and rolling over on their sides.

We stood up to signal back the news of what was happening, but the first flapping of the flags brought about our heads a storm of bullets. Our only chance was to run the message back through the enemy's barrage. The signaller started off down the trench. We waited for his return, but we waited in vain. A runner reached us from the company commander, asking for guns to be brought to bear upon a machine-gun nest which was holding up the advance. I had only Suzette left, so she took the message and vanished into the enemy barrage behind me. Shortly after she had gone on her errand another infantry-runner met me, with the message that our chaps had got through Fransart and were in sight of the railroad on the other side, but that the enemy machine-guns, which they thought they had demolished, were firing in their backs. None of my men had returned. I thought I knew why, for the ridge was boiling. There was no one left to send, so I set off to run the information back myself.

I have read in history of men who were never afraid, but I have not met their like at the front. All the men out here have been afraid and will be afraid again tomorrow. They acknowledge their fear, and conquer and despise it. The difference between the brave man and the coward is that, whereas the coward gives way to his imagination, the brave man carries on as if he were untouched by terror.

That day I was frankly afraid. As I entered the barrage every nerve in my body went on strike. Shells were exploding on the very lip of the trench; the shock of their concussion was like a blow aimed against my knee-joints. I felt blinded and faint. The smart of fumes was in my eyes; the reek in my throat was choking. I glanced across my shoulder to find that, where I had been standing a few seconds before, the trench had been blown up.

On in front across the part that I had to traverse, the grass was scorched and smoking. It was like being pummelled by a mob of invisible assassins. I staggered, and ran, and crawled, and panted; my heart was filled with hatred for the enemy miles behind at their guns, who bided their time and killed us at their leisure. Round each fresh traverse I expected to stumble across one of my men lying broken and sprawled out. Thinking that they might be in hiding I called their names again and again as I ran. I might just as well have called to the clouds in a storm at sea from a rowboat. I was mortally afraid that I should die alone. But beyond my terror was the sense of my obligation to those men up front, cut off from hope by the machine-guns firing in their backs; at any and every cost they must be helped.

CHAPTER 26

Death of Dan

I had reached the very heart of the barrage, when I felt a hand grabbing at my leg. I looked down and found two of my signallers and Suzette crouching in a hole which some infantry-men must have scooped for themselves. Had they not seized hold of me I should have gone past them, not knowing they were there. Bending down I shouted an enquiry as to whether they were wounded. They told me "No," but that it was impossible to signal since every time they tried to use their flags they brought a hail of lead about their heads; moreover, so long as the barrage lasted all the chain of signallers behind them were held hammered against the ground. There was no one to read their messages and it was probable that more than one of the receiving-stations had been wiped out. Realising the truth of what they said, I sat down beside them to recover my breath. While we sat there, as suddenly as the storm of death had broken, it lifted and leapt half a mile to the rear to about the line on which battalion headquarters were established.

Getting my party on to their legs, I arranged to send all my messages back to the ridge by runner and to have them relayed on from there out of sight of the enemy by flag-wagging. Taking one man with me and Suzette, since she knew Fransart well, I again pushed forward.

I got as far along the trench as to where the apple-trees crossed the road; there I halted. The enemy was putting up an intense bombardment just in rear of the village to prevent the approach of our reinforcements. It was now some time since any messages from the infantry up front had reached me; I began to get nervous lest something disastrous had happened. At last I determined to leave the man behind me to relay orders, and to go forward with Suzette. I had another reason for wishing to get into the village; I wanted to see if I could find any traces of Bully Beef and Dan. From where I was I could make out the spot where the Hun had stood up and beckoned to them. There was little chance that they were alive, but I was anxious to satisfy myself.

Watching our chance, Suzette and I popped out on to the roadway and commenced to run, crouching low and zigzagging. At once we became a target for the sharpshooters in the uncaptured village to our right flank. About our feet the dust began to go up in vicious spurts and about our heads we heard the sharp pizz-pizz of bullets. The intoxicating excitement of danger got into our blood; we called to each other and laughed as we ran.

God knows there was little enough to laugh about; of the company of a hundred and forty odd men who had attacked across that open space before us, upwards of a hundred were lying wounded and dead. But the curious psychology of battle is that no one ever thinks that other people's misfortunes may befall himself. While the wine of adventure sings in his head he believes himself immortal. That is the explanation of the boys who go cheering across the Tom-Tiddler's ground of death.

Breathless and still laughing we reached and jumped into what had been the Hun front-line. Here the laughter was wiped from our lips in a second. Everything was scared and silent. Our attack had not been expected; the enemy had been caught for fair. Our wall of fire had descended on him, shattered him, choked him, buried him. The troops in this part of the line had been Bavarians: jovial, fresh-complexioned, fair-haired men.

We knew them of old—genial fellows, with fine singing voices, who would exchange presents with you out in No Man's Land, and kill you treacherously while your present was still in their hands, without any consciousness of broken honour or unkindness. Here in the polluted summer quiet they lay in every contortion of distress, mangled, smashed and ended, their blue eyes wide open, staring at the sky and still retaining an expression of panic astonishment. They had come to war as we had come to war; but they had not expected to die. That was what they seemed to be telling us: "Take example from us; turn back in time."

We stumbled our way into a communication-trench, and hurried on, guessing at the direction our infantry must have taken. Here the brutality of what had happened was even more obvious; in the terror of their flight, the enemy had become jammed in the narrow space; they had fought with one another to escape and had trodden the wounded into the ground.

Now, following between the tunnelled roots of trees, we came to the village itself, lying in the heart of a little wood. The trench became so narrow that our equipment caught against its sides. Grass grew tall along its banks, and scattered through the grass were wildflowers. We had glimpses as we travelled of cottage gardens, beehives and curtained windows. But we were glad to keep our heads down, for shrapnel was stripping the leaves from the trees and bursting with the clash of cymbals above our heads. We were walking straight through our own barrage, and still there was no sign of our own infantry. We began to wonder whether we had gone beyond them or whether they had been all wiped out. Behind us in the houses of Fransart, which ought by rights to have been in our hands, we could hear the unmistakable cough of German machine-guns at work.

On the far side of the wood we stumbled on our men—twenty-six of them; all that were left. They were scattered at intervals along the trench, hugging the ground. As we stepped over them, going in search of their officer, they paid us no attention. They were most of them green troops—reinforcements, who were tasting the bitterness of battle for the first time. But so was Suzette; she showed no signs of faint-heartedness. Her eyes were gray stars, deep and quiet, and an eager smile played about her firm young mouth. In looking at her I was reminded of Joan of Arc, and could believe that she too had talked with heavenly presences.

Twenty-five yards ahead there was a trench-juncture, at which a lad was sitting with his legs wide apart and a scarlet hole bored through the centre of his forehead. No one had gone to his help; he merely sat there in the sunlight with a puzzled expression, watching the blood splash slowly on his hands. When I made to cross the trench-juncture, one of the men pulled me back. "A Hun sniper," he panted with an eloquent economy of words; "he gets everyone who goes there."

"But what's the matter with you chaps?" I asked.

"It's the booby-traps, sir," he said; "they've blown a lot of us up. We daren't stir."

Then I saw what he meant. Across the trench, beyond where the wounded man was sitting, cobwebs of wires had been strung a few inches above the ground, attached to pegs. They looked innocent enough, but were just at the right height to catch the feet of men advancing in single file. Should anyone trip against them, the jerk on the pegs would explode a series of mines.

I turned to the man. "Are you the furthest up of the attack?"

"Yes, sir."

"Do you know what's on ahead?"

"The railroad, sir, with a lot of freight-cars standing on the tracks. The Huns are hiding behind them and taking pot-shots at us."

Just then the company commander hove in sight, crouching low to avoid the sharp-shooters and stepping warily between the wires of the traps. While I spoke to him, Suzette was dragging the wounded lad back from the trench-juncture and binding up his head.

"A pretty rotten mess, I call it," the company commander growled pantingly, wiping the perspiration from his eyes. "We ought to have had tanks and aeroplanes to do this job and twice as many men. It's sheer murder. My men haven't a one *per cent* chance of coming out of the show alive; out of a hundred and forty I have twenty-six left. The enemy gets us from in front and from both flanks, while his machine-guns in Fransart are potting at our backs. And what the devil is our own artillery doing laying down a barrage behind us?"

The truth was the infantry had advanced too quickly, without first ascertaining that their gunners had been notified of their progress. They had also failed to "mop up" the enemy strongholds before pressing further forward. The consequence was that they had left pockets of resistance on every hand and that their own artillery was cutting them off from help. Their situation was desperate.

There was only one remedy; to find out the exact locations of the machine-gun nests and to send the information back to the guns, that they might knock them out with high explosive; to send back orders to our artillery that the barrage should be raised; and to withdraw our troops from Fransart and subject the village to a fresh bombardment. But to what place could we safely withdraw our infantry while the bombardment was in progress—that was the question. To answer this question the company commander and I decided that a further reconnaissance was necessary. We did not know what lay on ahead or how near to us the Huns were; at all events, it could not be much more dangerous further forward.

Leaving instructions that the men should keep well under cover to avoid casualties in our absence, we set out. Treading gingerly up the trench mined with booby-traps, we came to. a turning which led off to the right. Here things were comparatively quiet, all the firing passing well above our heads. We followed the turning for about two hundred yards, and then peered stealthily over the top. Not fifty yards away was the railroad, with the freight-cars either standing on the tracks or thrown over on their sides to form a barrier. Poking out from loopholes, which had been cut in the woodwork, were the muzzles of rifles. We had seen all that was necessary; we knew that we must take a gambler's chance. I arranged with the company commander that he should lead his men still further forward to this trench so that they might be clear of our shell-fire, and that he should see to the warning of our infantry who were in Fransart, while I ran the orders back to the guns and saw to it that reinforcements were sent up the moment our bombardment ended.

The return journey to the signalling-station where the apple-trees crossed the road, was as hot a piece of work as I remember. Suzette took it as coolly as if it were no more than a country-walk. We had to pass through both our own barrage and the enemy's. Of the two ours was the worse. In Fransart itself the trench had been made more shallow by direct hits with shells. As we wriggled our way on hands and knees over debris, we could see the Hun machine-gunners blazing away from the attics of houses and our own men crawling through the undergrowth to rush the entrances with bombs. I remember discussing with my conscience the decency of permitting Suzette to run such risks. But I had no choice, for if I were killed, she might survive to get the messages back; in any case, when she learnt about Bully Beef, she would receive her death-warrant.

We found our signaller where we had left him and at once got him to work flag-wagging the information to the rear. The enemy spotted him after the first few minutes; but with a reckless disregard for his own safety, he carried on amid a hail of bullets till the task was ended. A quarter of an hour later, like a hurricane let loose, the levelling of Fransart commenced. The wood rocked as in a gale.

Roofs were stripped from the houses; the walls shuddered and knelt slowly down like camels. This concentrated commotion was intensified for us by the contrast of the breathless stillness of the surrounding country. For myself I was picturing the wild scramble for life of the Huns whom we had seen firing from the windows of the attics. They were brave men, who had purposed to sell their lives dearly. To kill them without giving them a chance, in a way which they had not anticipated, was fair; but its fairness did not make it less appallingly dramatic.

I was roused from these thoughts by a trembling at my side; it came from Suzette. She was kneeling with her face cushioned in her hands and was weeping violently. I bent over her, asking what was the matter. "Eet was my 'ome," she said.

Suddenly she leapt to her feet and stood tiptoe, staring. I followed her gaze. Out of the wood where trees were crashing and the ground was billowing itself into mounds, two men were advancing. They walked gropingly and the arm of the taller was flung about the other's neck. The taller man was wounded and in khaki; his companion was a plump little Bavarian—evidently one of the machine-gunners who had been firing in our backs. Every now and then we lost them as a shell burst in their path; but always they emerged through the smoke of the bombardment, dragging themselves by inches nearer to the comparative safety that was ours. Without a word of warning, Suzette burst from me and commenced to race towards them. It was sheer foolishness to venture into that inferno where every second seemed to be a man's last. I started after her, intending if need be to hold her back by force.

As I drew nearer, I saw what her sharp eyes had discerned already, that the wounded man carried a child against his breast; then I recognized who he was. At that moment he pitched forward, pulling the Bavarian with him to the ground. When the enemy had tottered slowly to his feet, he rose alone and had transferred the child to his own arms. But Suzette had reached him now; she snatched the child to her body. Like a drama played out, the last shell fell and the bombardment was ended.

I glanced behind me. Like a winding stream, following the serpentine wanderings of the trench, I saw the gleaming bayonets of our reinforcements shining above the tangled grass. Five minutes later when I re-entered the ravished wood, guiding up the supports to a new attack, I passed Suzette. She had forgotten that she was dressed in khaki. She sat among the debris of splintered trees mothering Bully Beef, who was quite unhurt, while the plump little Bavarian smiled down on her in mild astonishment. At full length lay Dan, his old soldier's face composed and kindly—his last fight ended. He had had his desire, as so often expressed in his favourite song: his duty accomplished, he had simply "faded."

CHAPTER 27

More Night Marches

It is many days since I wrote the last line. This battle goes on and on. We are drunk for want of sleep and rest. How much farther can we drive these weary bodies of ours without their collapsing? We treat them as things of naught—as mere slaves whom we lash in action to carry our spirits forward. We do not wash them, feed them, clothe them with any care; we scarcely spare the time to keep them alive while the victory is so nearly within our grasp. It is amazing that such a multitude of diverse men should be agreed to have so little mercy on themselves.

One feels that there are two armies fighting, for every one that is apparent: the external, sullen army of heavy-eyed, red-rimmed flesh, and the invisible, eager, clear-eyed army of indestructible souls, which flogs the laggard army of the flesh forward. Behind us, all along the battlefields of the advance, the earth of men lies mouldering and putrescent, but their liberated spirits still fight beside our spirits, treading close upon the heels of the enemy.

The test of scarlet! We used to speak about it, but we never dreamt that it could be such a test. We never knew that human mechanisms could survive such ordeals and be patched up with courage to endure them afresh.

After the capturing of Fransart our corps was drawn out and French troops were thrown in to hold the line which we had broken. Then the terrible night-marches recommenced, for the enemy must not know where we were going. Again we must play the game of hiding, and vanish entirely. We must be the will-o'-the-wisps of the Western Front and disclose ourselves unheralded at a point where we were least expected. We ourselves must have no knowledge of our destination; our job must be to move like ghosts and to cover as much ground as possible under the shadow of darkness.

At the end of the first stage we concealed ourselves in woods, which had in a day become familiar to all the English-speaking world. It was here that our cavalry surrounded an entire German cavalry division, entrained and on the point of pulling out. It was here that our infantry captured a Hun hospital, and set an example in chivalry by offering the nurses the choice between working for our wounded or a safe conduct to the lines of their own countrymen. It was here that Big Bertha was found—the long-range maneater which had tried to murder Paris. But, sweetest of all memories, it was here, after the long drought, that the rain descended and we stripped off our clothes, stiff as boards with sweat, and ran naked through the leaves in the stinging downpour.

On the evening of the second stage we passed through wheatfields, recently recaptured from the enemy, still strewn with Australia's unburied dead. Here troops were busily at work gathering in the harvest of the trampled grain. We realised then that it was not our blood alone, willingly as it was shed, that would restore peace and happiness to the world, but the thrift that could satisfy man's bitter cry for bread.

How many marches did we make? How often did we rest? I cannot remember now. What happened is all a blur. We crawled across a devastated land through a fog of moonlight, dawns and sunsets. We gave and obeyed orders mechanically. Our perceptions were dulled; we were mad for sleep. As soon as our eyes closed, the relentless word would go round to harness up and move on, always to move on; but to what were we marching?

It seemed as though all the world were dead and we were the only fighters left. Though the light failed and one could scarcely see his hand before his face, we knew by the heavy staleness in the air that we were traversing interminable graveyards, where villages, trees, men and horses lay shallowly beneath the swollen sod. And yet we knew that there were other fighters besides ourselves. How the rumour reached us I cannot tell, but we were aware that the Americans were massing before St. Mihiel, and that they were piled up in their thousands behind Ypres.

Long after the graciousness of sleep had come to us, they would tramp in their millions above our quiet beds; we should feel the pressure of their heels upon our foreheads and should know that they were carrying on our work. It didn't matter what happened to us; the work of victory would go on just the same. The Hun would not triumph. We should not have spent our youth in vain. In this knowledge, despite our weariness, we were glad.

I have a curious feeling that on those long night-marches I held conversations with men, with whom I certainly scarcely exchanged a word. At all events, though I did not speak to them, I knew what was happening inside their heads. Perhaps it was that we had all become abnormal with the strain and developed a mental telepathy which communicated thoughts without the fatigue of words.

As we moved through the darkness it was as though each brain was a little lighted house, behind whose windows shadows came and went. I knew, for instance, what Trottot was thinking. He was brooding over his failure to disprove his reputation for being yellow. He was resentful of his sergeant who had kept him back at the wagon-lines whenever the shell-fire was intense up front. He was hungering for the chance to do something so reckless that everyone would have to vote him brave enough to be lead-driver of the gun. I knew what the major was thinking: at the head of the column he was thinking unceasingly of Suzette. And Heming, bringing up the rear with the transport, he was thinking of two women and hoping that the next fight would be his last.

Sometimes I had the odd sensation that there were many more marching with the battery than would ever again answer the roll-call. I was riding at the head of my section half asleep about midnight, when a horseman came up at the gallop and reined in beside me. I expected to hear him deliver some message; instead he dropped into a walk at my side. His steel helmet shadowed his face. I was too weary to speak unnecessarily and took him for one of my sergeants.

Perhaps I drowsed; when I again noticed him the moon was coming out from under cloud. Then I saw that he was wearing an officer's uniform. That piqued me into wakefulness. I leant forward to get a closer glimpse of his features. As I did so, he flung his horse back on its haunches, wheeled to the left and vanished in the dark. During the brief space while I gazed on him, I recognized Tubby Grain.

Other men in the battery are telling similar stories. They have seen Big Dan, Standish and many of their fallen comrades. They ride on the limbers and the wagons; they plod persistently behind the guns. They do not seek to attract attention to themselves. They do not talk or inconvenience anybody. Having died in a foreign land, it seems normal and right that their spirits should still accompany us. At dawn they vanish. As regards Tubby Grain, since the first time I have never seen his face—only his plump little figure going at the trot through the darkness down the column.

And now our marches are, for the time being, at an end. Once again we have been flung in as the hammerhead of the attack. They say that Foch's principle is to use up his storm-troops; he never relieves them when once an offensive has begun. We no longer guess—we know the task that lies before us. Last time it was the saving of Amiens; this time it is the breaking of the Hindenburg Line. Two nights ago we pulled into action across the bald chalky country that straddles the Cambrai-Arras road.

To the north of us, rising out of the blackness of the Vimy Plain, we could see the ridge which was so long our home and which, because we were not allowed to die, we guarded with so much impatience. Ah, how impatient we were while the indignity of not dying was upon us! How little we valued the supreme gift of life! How we courted death in raid after raid throughout the summer! Had we known then how few sunny days remained for most of us, how much more gratefully we should have lived them. We have come back for what will probably be our severest test to very nearly the spot whence we started.

Nobody now garrisons what was once regarded as the Gibraltar of the Western Front. Our armies have swept forward like a tidal wave and are beating on the doors of the cities in the plain, which a month ago looked so distant and impregnable.

Our brigade has been pushed well up into the point of a narrow salient—a long thin cape of recaptured territory which projects far out into the enemy country. We are so far up that the Hun balloons are actually in rear of us and watch our every movement from either flank. Any time that they choose they can bring accurate fire to bear on us. We have been in some murder-holes before, but this is by long adds the worst. The Hun game is to obliterate us before we get started. All day and all night he bombards us without cessation. When high explosives have failed, he drenches us with gas.

Now that we are here there is no use in trying to disguise either our presence or our purpose. The old subterfuge of camouflage is of no avail. The country is too bare and too much overlooked for any precautions, however ingenious, to protect us. Our only chance is to hurry up and get the attack begun before we are all dead. There will be a percentage of safety when we begin to go forward; there is none in sitting still. That we may launch our offensive quickly, we are making every effort.

No man's life is precious. Guns and ammunition drive up in the broad daylight and are knocked out. No sooner are they knocked out than others are sent forward to take their places. The waste is stupendous. Direct hits are scored on ammunition-dumps; there is never an hour when explosives cannot be seen going up in flames—never an hour when horses and men cannot be seen rolling in their final agony. The spectacle is too ordinary to excite us. We are too much fatalists to be intimidated. With a misleading display of callousness, while the unlucky are dying, we who are whole carry on with our preparations for revenge, which the enemy watching from the sky does his utmost to prevent.

Our battery is in a narrow valley to the left of what was once a town. A sign-board, with the name painted on it, is its only means of identification: "This was a town." It is the same with all the sites of former human habitation which lie behind us; if it were not for the sign-boards, they would be indistinguishable from the miles of shell-ploughed waste and mine-craters in which this abomination of desolation abounds. The country as far as eye can search, lies stark and evil as an alkali desert.

In our valley there is a stagnant malodorous swamp, close to which we have dragged in our guns so that their muzzles point out across it. It was once a river winding through a pleasant meadow, but gradually it has become choked by the refuse of dead things—dead men, dead horses, dead happiness. God knows what it hides. It has been kind to us, nevertheless, for it has saved us many casualties. All the enemy's rounds which fall short of us plunge harmlessly into the liquid mud. We hear them coming with the roar of express engines. We make a bet where they are going to burst. Then a column of filth goes up from the swamp and we know that this slough of despond has again preserved us.

If we have been lucky, others have been less fortunate. The valley being stiff with batteries, there are not enough good positions to go round. One watches the shells alight, then sees the men rushing for stretchers. In an endless chain the ammunition-wagons drive up, fling out their rounds and depart at the gallop. Let them move quickly and ever more quickly, there are always some of them that get caught. The place is rapidly becoming a shambles. No one's life is worth a minute's purchase. It would be interesting to know what premium we should have to pay if we wanted to insure ourselves.

The major has just told me that the attack is to be launched tomorrow at dawn. It's extraordinarily ambitious, for its third objective is fifteen thousand yards from where we are at present, and it's ultimate goal is the capture of Cambrai. Between ourselves and Cambrai stretches the most strongly fortified country of the entire German front—a country naturally fortified by marshes and canals and made doubly impregnable by military cunning. The Hindenburg Line will have to be taken first before any general advance can be begun. After that certain sacrifice-tanks will go through and drown themselves in the canals to make a bridge over which the living tanks and cavalry may push forward to conquest.

We can stand any amount of pummelling now that we know the worst. It's going to be a top-hole show—"Berlin or nothing;" those were the major's words. Judging by the pleased grins on the men's faces, it won't be nothing. We're going to finish the job this time and be done with it forever. Since the men have heard the news, they've generated quite a "home for Christmas" air of jollity. There is only one man who looks sad—Captain Heming. He has received orders to start for Blighty at once to give evidence in the case of Mrs. Dragott.

"Don't go if you don't want to," said the major. "I'll stand by you if there's trouble. Please yourself."

We're wondering how he'll decide. It depends on his evidence, whether it would save or condemn her.

If it would condemn her and he still loves her——A man can live worse deaths than falling honourably in battle.

CHAPTER 28

Taking a Blighty

It is wonderful to lie here in the quiet and to know that it is all ended. Already the world is saying, "Let's forget that there was a war." That's natural for people fatigued by contemplating tragedy; but which is the more inconvenient—to have been a spectator or an endurer of tragedy? It's all very well for the spectators to say, "It's over, thank God. We're safe now, let's go home and be gay as we once were." But how can we, who were comrades in the ordeal, ever forget? And the rest of the world which only watched from afar, what right has it to forget? Now that it has been saved by other men's loss, is it its obligations that it would forget? Would it forget the pain which our bodies will always remember? Would it forget the cold, the thirst, the weariness, the wounds, the forlornness, the despairing courage which it did not share? Would it forget the dead who forewent their gladness, believing that their immortality was secured by the gratitude which would commemorate their simple heroism?

If it does forget, it absconds like a blackguard debtor, cheating both us and the dead. For we fought not for victory alone, but to establish a loftier standard, so that the world in recalling the price we paid might make itself kinder and better. As I lie here in hospital, six stories up, with the throb of London beating distantly like a receding drum beneath my window, I am sometimes uncertain whether any of the scenes I have lived through ever happened. The war grows unreal and vague. Surely those ex-plumbers, ex-bricklayers, ex-piano-tuners with whom

I marched, are only imagined. At this distance it seems incredible that such men should have found the fortitude to make themselves the knights of Armageddon.

They were so ordinary, so ignorant of their true greatness, so blind to the magnanimous courage of their martyrdom. Ordinary, ignorant and blind they were; perhaps their indifference to their worth was their outstanding glory. Yet these everyday men proved not by ones or twos, but in their millions that the spirit of righteous freedom only slumbers. In remembering their example never again can we believe ourselves ignoble or that the race of sacrificial men is ever ended.

My little major, with the V. C. ribbon on his breast, came on leave from Mons the other day and hopped in, merry as ever, to see me. He was at the front when the Armistice was declared; I was eager to hear about it. "How did the men take it?" I asked him.

"Like any other happening," he said.

"But wasn't there any excitement or cheering?"

"There may have been, but I didn't see it," he told me. " We were marching up to a fresh attack when the word reached us. We halted and drew in to the side of the road, feeling a trifle discontented on account of the cold. One felt warmer, you understand, while in motion. It was a raw day, being November. When the news had been confirmed, we turned back to the last town in search of billets. The chaps cracked a smile then, when they discovered that they were to have a solid night's rest with a roof above their heads."

I levered myself up in bed and stared at Charlie Wraith. Despite all that I knew of the Front, I found it hard to credit this utter lack of emotion. In the old days all our talk had been of when the war would end—how we would throw aside authority, cock our guns up and fire off salvo after salvo to the heavens. We had promised ourselves that we would go over the top for a last time as a kind of sporting luxury, and beat up the Hun just once more for luck to prove that we still had plenty of ginger left. The flying-men had asserted that they would head their planes in the direction of Boche-land and send them off unpiloted to put the wind up the enemy. Every mad prank had been imagined and discussed for making our celebration memorable and effective. From the Channel to Switzerland the front should blaze and be clangourous. And this was actually how the greatest war in history had fizzled out: they had drawn in to the side of the road, felt cold and turned back to the nearest town in search of billets. Had the major told me that the men had shewn resentment, feeling that they had been baulked of an immenser victory, I could have understood that But this account of stoical indifference was astounding. I tried to put some of my surprise into words.

"If they weren't glad, perhaps they were disappointed?"

"Not disappointed," he said. "We'd been through too much to be either happy or sad. I think we'd got past feeling anything. We were sort of numb. I'm no good at expressing myself. Some of the married chaps sighed contentedly and whispered, more to themselves than aloud, 'Well, that's that.' They meant, I suppose, that they'd be seeing their wives again presently. But most of us didn't say a word; we just carried on as if nothing out of the ordinary had occurred."

I think this picture of dumb subjection to duty made me realise more than anything the sheer cost of victory in spiritual energy to the men who bought it with their blood. While London, New York and Paris went mad, climbing lamp-posts, changing hats, dragging tin cans through the streets and converting themselves into impromptu jazz bands, these men, whose valour was being commemorated, pulled in to the side of the road, felt cold, and limped back to the nearest town in search of billets.

They were "sort of numb." They'd been through too much to feel either happy or sad. "Well, that's that," they had said, and thanked God for the luxury of a secure night's rest and the comfort of a roof above their heads.

And yet, why I should have been so surprised I don't quite know. The major's picture was consistent with everything I had learned of the fighting man—precisely what one might have expected. That I should have been surprised only proves to me how thoroughly normal and civilian we are beneath our khaki. Here am I, a few weeks out of the line, finding myself amazed at conduct which would have been mine, had I lasted.

"Well, that's that"—it sums up in a phrase the whole philosophy of the Front, which teaches:—"Don't whine. Endure what you can't alter. Get over the hard bits of the road by pushing forward. Never know when you're licked. Never be elated when you've won. Whether you win or lose, don't sit down; seize on to the next most difficult thing that you may conquer. For it's not the winning or the losing, it's the eternal trying that counts—And that's that."

It is the "eternal trying" of my last fight that lives most vividly in my memory. We were in that murder-hole, you will remember, to the left of the Cambrai-Arras road. Our job was to smash the Hindenburg Line and to go as much further as our strength would carry us. Our objective was to be the ending of the war or, in the words of the major, "Berlin or nothing."

The night before the show the enemy made a last determined effort to knock us out. We had distinct orders not to retaliate; our first round was to be fired with the opening of the offensive. So we had to lie down in silence and take our punishment.

Shortly after sunset the trouble commenced. The enemy must have run forward a number of guns. Without warning a tremendous bombardment opened up. It was as though the walls of Heaven were tumbling about our heads. In our narrow valley, where batteries were lined up like taxi-cabs on a stand, shells of every kind and calibre began to fall—whizz-bangs, incendiary, high explosive, gas. Shooting at random over so small an area so densely packed, it was almost impossible not to hit something.

As darkness thickened, the night became lurid with burning gun-pits and ammunition. Against the dancing flames men could be seen, running, gesticulating and working like fiends to put the fires out. High above the whistling of the shells we heard the ominous throb of planes, and bombs commenced dropping. By this time we had struggled into our gas-helmets and lay crouched in little groups in the bottom of shell-holes. We were of no use. We had been forbidden to reply. We were simply waiting to be slaughtered.

I don't know what happened at the other batteries, but our major took matters into his own hands. "We shall have no men left for tomorrow at this rate," he said; so he ordered the chaps to get out of the bombarded area and to scatter. The instructions for the attack had just come in, and he had to make out the barrage-tables. To do this it would be necessary to light a candle, but it would be suicide to show any lights while the planes were over-head. Seizing his fighting map and scales, he retired in search of a dugout; soon only I and one signaller were left. We had to remain on the position to answer the 'phone and to keep in touch with the rear.

We lay there hugging the ground. We had had no time to build overhead protection; the weather being warm, we had contented ourselves with digging holes three feet deep and spreading over them ground-sheets to keep the rain out. Our sensations were those of men who were lying on an erupting volcano. The earth quivered under us and the air was thick with the avalanche of falling debris. The valves of our gasmasks felt choked with dust; we were well-nigh suffocated and buried. The ground-sheets above our heads flapped in rags. Stones and bits of chalk, thrown up by the concussion, bruised us. We were always expecting that the next shell would end us. They came over with the galloping thud of cavalry, *ker-plunk, ker-plunk, ker-plunk.* The roars of the explosions, which followed the thuds of impact, were like the fierce ha-has of ten thousand maniacs.

It was long past midnight before the strafe died down. By that time the Hun felt fairly confident that few, if any of us, had survived. One by one, through the altered landscape, our men crept back. By the red glow of dying conflagrations, they set patiently to work to clean their guns and set their fuses, so that all might be ready for revenge. We did not number them as they returned. It was impossible in the darkness, but we knew by the spattered human fragments that in the surrounding shell-holes many a stout fellow had gone west.

A little whiteness spread along the eastern horizon. We stared at our luminous wrist-watches. The second-hand had one more revolution to travel. The whistle sounded; our turn had come. If the enemy had supposed that he had exterminated us, his disillusionment must have been bitter. There were batteries which he had crippled, but none that he had silenced. Like fiery serpents, even from where we were, we could see our bursting shrapnel hissing down on his tormented trenches.

And now, when it was too late, he made a furious effort to complete our destruction. He tried to bury us beneath the weight of metal that he sent racing through the semi-darkness. Men and guns were blotted out by the dust of explosions; but the whistle for each new lift in the barrage went on sounding. It seemed a miracle that our shells did not collide with his in mid-air.

His anger was not for long. Of a sudden, from intensity it died down into nothing. We knew what that meant: the bayonets of our infantry were tossing human hay in his trenches, our heavy artillery was raking his batteries, and our tanks were going forward, tracking down their prey like blood-hounds.

Dawn strengthened. From a shadowy hint of whiteness it became a pillar of flame, from a pillar of flame a shaft of dazzling brightness. We gazed on the night's work. It was as though a gigantic plough had furrowed the valley from end to end. Guns leaned over on their axles with their wheels smashed; the men who should have been serving them lay scattered about, half buried and scarcely recognisable. Charred piles of ammunition smoked lazily and occasionally sputtered like damp fire-works. We marvelled how we had escaped; all the guns of our battery were still in action. Again it must have been the swamp that had saved them.

We could estimate the progress that our infantry were making by the orders to lengthen our range, which we kept receiving across the 'phone. They were going very rapidly. The enemy resistance could not have been as strong as had been expected. We judged that the first wave of our attack must be almost through the Hindenburg Line. Soon it would be necessary for us to hook in and move forward if we were not to get out of touch.

It was eight o'clock when our teams arrived with Heming riding at their head. None of us commented on his presence. He had disobeyed the summons to England and was taking one last chance in battle of maintaining his silence forever. We knew then that the woman whom he had loved was guilty—that whatever he could have said would have told against her. His face had a sterner expression than I had ever seen it wear; it looked gray and haggard. Only his eyes had their steady gaze of untroubled brave resolution. He rode up to the major and reported the number of the men and horses killed and wounded that night at the wagon-lines. "It was the bombing planes did it," he said; "they were right on top of us. We're short of gunners now, so I had to bring Suzette."

Then he took his instructions and rode back to the teams to keep them out of shell-fire till they were needed.

An hour went by. The major had got mounted and gone forward to a windmill, just behind the furthest point of our attack, from where he could watch developments and send back for us the moment we were required. He was determined this time to be in the thick of it. His last words had been that, if our headquarters tried to hold us back, we were to let our wires to the rear go down and obey him only; he would be answerable.

Already several batteries had hooked in and disappeared over the crest at the gallop. We were beginning to feel impatient and fearful lest once again we were to see very little of the fun, when the major's orderly came in sight taking shell-holes like a steeple-chaser. Pulling his horse up on its haunches, he delivered a written message:

Our infantry have broken the Hindenburg Line, but the enemy are massed behind it. They've led our chaps into a trap and are putting up their real fight in their support-trenches. Our tanks have gone on and cannot help. Much of our artillery fire is at too long range to be effective.

Close support is absolutely necessary. Our infantry are being pushed back. Move the battery up by sections, Captain Heming taking the leading section and you the rear, with an interval of at least ten minutes between them. We are practically in sight of the Boche, so leave twenty yards between your guns and wagons. It's a sacrifice job, so expect a hot time. My orderly will show Captain Heming where to come into action.

Heming came up just as I had finished reading the crumpled slip of paper. I handed it to him. He glanced it through in silence. His face broke into a smile. "It may be death," he said.

He signalled for his teams to come up. While they were hooking in, he spoke with me quietly. "Once on the Somme I asked you to give a message to a lady if I were wiped out. I wasn't; but I may be today. If that happens, I want you to give her the same message. Tell her that I did everything that she might feel proud of our friendship."

He met my eye and looked away. "In years to come she'll need something to make her feel proud, so don't spoil it. Don't tell her about Suzette. But you chaps, however many of you are left—you'll take care of Suzette. I know that!"

"We'll take care of Suzette," I said.

"And my message ?"

"I'll deliver your message."

The guns were pulling out. I watched them file off round the swamp, followed by their ammunition-wagons. When the last wagon was clear, Heming waved his hand to me.

"Good luck," I shouted.

He galloped off to the head of the column. Then I noticed that someone was running to catch up behind. For a moment I thought it was a gunner of the detachments; then I recognised Suzette. They went at the walk across the valley; as they neared the top of the crest on the other side, shells began to burst. They were now a target for the enemy, and broke into first the trot and then the gallop. In a cloud of dust and smoke they disappeared from sight. Ten minutes later the centre section went forward. About fifteen minutes after that I pulled out, taking with me the remaining section. I glanced back at my men. We'd been in tight corners before together. I would take a bet on how they would be-have. Among them all there was only one query-mark—Driver Trottrot. He was riding lead of one of the first-line wagons. If he'd got over his fear of shell-fire, within the next hour he would have his chance to prove it.

There was only one road by which to climb the crest; it had been well advertised by the other batteries. As we reached the top, we were skeletoned against the sky-line and hell broke loose about us. Setting spurs to our horses, we went off at the wild tear. With the vehicles swaying and thundering behind us, we passed over the first line of resistance, which our infantry had captured that morning. The air was heavy with the smell of gas, but worse than the gas were the incendiary shells, which sent up showers of liquid fire where they struck, maddening the horses.

On account of the trench-systems it was impossible to go across the open country, so we had to bear to the right and come down on to the Cambrai-Arras road. It was crowded with transport—tanks, pontoons and lorries full of engineers, being rushed up to bridge and hold the canals in the belief that the attack was still going ahead. We had to slow down to the crawl in places. The road was a sure target for the enemy; he knew that it was our one means of advance and, consequently, gave it constant attention. One vehicle struck caused a block in the traffic for half a mile; men worked furiously among the falling shells to drag the cripples to one side. In the ditches, where they had fallen that morning, dead horses and men, both the enemy's and ours, lay crushed and crumpled.

No one wished to pay heed to them; we did our utmost to ignore them as though they were utterly negligible. But they seemed to cry out to us, appealing for our pity; then, when we shuddered, threatening us with the same terrifying, uncared-for Nemesis. When we let our eyes rest on them they were lying harmless and quiet, but we had the feeling that behind our backs they sat up with their wounds gaping, and gnawed their fists at us. Our animals shied at the corpses, breaking into a sweat and becoming un-manageable. If the dead were not a sufficient warning of what war could do to us, there was always the crimson returning tide of battered men, washing grievously past us back to Arras like a stream of blood.

Patriotism and glory! They sounded empty words compared with life. There was only one word that was an incentive to keep us steady—pride. We might survive; we did not wish to live with selves who would have to hang their heads. Yes, and there was another incentive—duty: the thought of comrades still further forward, to whom the roar of our eighteen-pounders would be happy as a peal of bells.

Crawling, halting, trotting for brief spells, we had travelled about four thousand yards when we saw the windmill on the rise, from which the major was observing, and in front of the windmill the Hindenburg Line which we were supposed to have smashed. In the plain which stretched behind the mill, our sacrifice batteries were strung out, belching fire. Across the plain our supporting infantry were trickling up in Indian file, winding their way about the batteries in action and side-stepping to avoid the bursting shells.

Suddenly we understood, as though the meaning of what for four years we had been doing were being revealed to us for the first time. In a flash we saw war's glory, its wickedness, magnanimity, challenge and the amazing fortitude it begets in men. It taught unbrave, ordinary chaps how to try and go on trying, long after hope seemed at an end. Each one of those batteries out there in the plain was Like a "Little Revenge," surrounded and dragged down by weight of numbers; but out of sheer self-respecting stubbornness it never ceased spurting fire. Everyone of those infantry, plodding stolidly forward, was quaking at the thought of the judgement day up front; but each one of them would rather die a thousand deaths than shew the white-feather. The sight was blinding, maddening, intoxicating. If those chaps didn't mind dying, why should we hang on to life?

Leaving the first-line wagons parked by the road-side, we

set off at the gallop with the guns and firing-battery wagons to where we saw Heming's four guns blazing away in the sunshine. The infantry stood aside to give us passage. They waved their caps and shouted. We could not hear a word of what they said; we only saw their lips moving. The pounding of our going drowned all other sounds.

We swung into line on Heming's right, flinging our horses back on their haunches. Before we had had time to unhook, a shell had burst directly under the centre team of A. Sub's gun; men and horses were rolling. We dragged our drivers out and had to shoot the horses before we could get the gun into action. Then bedlam broke loose.

Whether it was that the enemy had seen the heads of our horsemen above the rise and had got the line on us over open sights, or whether he had seen the flash of Heming's firing before we had come up, we could not tell. In any case he was upon us now. All along the line of guns his hurricane of shells began to burst. They fell on top and plus and minus of us. shutting us off from help. From our wagon-lines on the roadside our peril had been sized up and teams were coming at the gallop to drag us out.

They never got as far as us. Two hundred yards short, as though he had been potting at them with a rifle, the enemy caught them, and they crashed and sank in a cloud of dust. No sooner were they down than fresh teams dashed out. By his riding I recognised the lead-driver of the foremost team as Trottrot. At last his opportunity had come. He was winning his spurs and proving to all the watching world that he was not yellow. He would never reach us. He was riding towards certain and useless death. He was almost in the storm-centre, when I ran out and signalled him back.

In the middle of the battery, as cool and collected as if nothing were happening, Heming sat, his map-board on his knees. Suzette knelt beside him, doing his pencilling and listening through the 'phone to the directions of the major from up front. Now and then he looked up to give his orders for new ranges and angles; the expression on his face was triumphant. Every so often he left his map-board and walked among the men, encouraging them, "Stick to it, boys. We've got to blow the enemy out of the wire. It won't take much longer now."

But the boys were growing fewer. There were less and less of us to hear him every time he spoke to us. Three guns had been knocked out, and their crews were lying dead about them. Now there were only two left; now only one.

Suzette was setting fuses. Heming was loading and putting on the ranges. I was laying and firing. We were all three wounded. We three had taken the places of the dead gunners and seemed to have been going through these motions, alone and mechanically, keeping the remaining gun in action, ever since eternity had begun.

Something happened to end it—a roar, a sheet of flame; then darkness.

A stream of warmth was trickling down my face and neck. I opened my eyes. The gun was lying over on its side; like worshippers at mass, Heming and Suzette were kneeling with clasped hands, their faces towards the red altar of the enemy. As I watched, their faces drew together and his arm went about her. Their action became symbolic; it was like England greeting France in the hour of agony.

Everything faded. The shock and clamour drifted into silence. The test of scarlet was ended.

Here in the white orderliness of a sheeted bed, with the accustomedness of peace on every hand, it is strange to remember.

LEONAUR

ALSO FROM LEONAUR

AVAILABLE IN SOFTCOVER OR HARDCOVER WITH DUST JACKET

CAPTAIN OF THE 95th (Rifles) *by Jonathan Leach*—An officer of Wellington's Sharpshooters during the Peninsular, South of France and Waterloo Campaigns of the Napoleonic Wars.

BUGLER AND OFFICER OF THE RIFLES *by William Green & Harry Smith* With the 95th (Rifles) during the Peninsular & Waterloo Campaigns of the Napoleonic Wars

BAYONETS, BUGLES AND BONNETS *by James 'Thomas' Todd*—Experiences of hard soldiering with the 71st Foot - the Highland Light Infantry - through many battles of the Napoleonic wars including the Peninsular & Waterloo Campaigns

THE ADVENTURES OF A LIGHT DRAGOON *by George Farmer & G.R. Gleig*—A cavalryman during the Peninsular & Waterloo Campaigns, in captivity & at the siege of Bhurtpore, India

THE COMPLEAT RIFLEMAN HARRIS *by Benjamin Harris as told to & transcribed by Captain Henry Curling*—The adventures of a soldier of the 95th (Rifles) during the Peninsular Campaign of the Napoleonic Wars

WITH WELLINGTON'S LIGHT CAVALRY *by William Tomkinson*—The Experiences of an officer of the 16th Light Dragoons in the Peninsular and Waterloo campaigns of the Napoleonic Wars.

SURTEES OF THE RIFLES *by William Surtees*—A Soldier of the 95th (Rifles) in the Peninsular campaign of the Napoleonic Wars.

ENSIGN BELL IN THE PENINSULAR WAR *by George Bell*—The Experiences of a young British Soldier of the 34th Regiment 'The Cumberland Gentlemen' in the Napoleonic wars.

WITH THE LIGHT DIVISION *by John H. Cooke*—The Experiences of an Officer of the 43rd Light Infantry in the Peninsula and South of France During the Napoleonic Wars

NAPOLEON'S IMPERIAL GUARD: FROM MARENGO TO WATERLOO *by J. T. Headley*—This is the story of Napoleon's Imperial Guard from the bearskin caps of the grenadiers to the flamboyance of their mounted chasseurs, their principal characters and the men who commanded them.

BATTLES & SIEGES OF THE PENINSULAR WAR *by W. H. Fitchett*—Corunna, Busaco, Albuera, Ciudad Rodrigo, Badajos, Salamanca, San Sebastian & Others

www.ingramcontent.com/pod-product-compliance
Lightning Source LLC
Chambersburg PA
CBHW032053080426
42733CB00006B/258